God's Plan For You

By
Rick Layton

VINCOM, Inc.
Tulsa, Oklahoma

Unless otherwise indicated, all Scripture quotations are taken from the *King James Version* of the Bible.

Scripture quotations marked "NAS" are taken from the *New American Standard Bible.* Copyright © 1960, 1962, 1963, 1968, 1971, 1972, 1973, 1975, 1977 by The Lockman Foundation, La Habra, California.

Scripture quotations marked "AMP." are taken from *The Amplified Bible, New Testament,* copyright © 1954, 1958 by The Lockman Foundation, La Habra, California, or from *The Amplified Bible, Old Testament,* copyright © 1962, 1964 by Zondervan Publishing House, Grand Rapids, Michigan.

Scripture quotations marked "NIV" are taken from *The Holy Bible: New International Version.* Copyright © 1973, 1978, 1984 by the International Bible Society. Used by permission of Zondervan Bible Publishers, Grand Rapids, Michigan.

Scripture quotations marked "TLB" are taken from *The Living Bible.* Copyright © 1971 by Tyndale House Publishers, Inc., Wheaton, Illinois.

God's Plan For You
ISBN 0-927936-41-0

P. O. Box 17858
Shreveport, LA 71138

Published by VINCOM, Inc.
P. O. Box 702400
Tulsa, OK 74170

Contents

Introduction

Some time ago, I read a book by Van Crouch. In this particular book, there were two quotations that struck me as true.

The first quotation was, *''He who expects little will not be disappointed.''* This is very true. People with no purpose in life get nowhere. If you and I are to accomplish anything for ourselves, our families, or for the Kingdom of God, we must have specific goals in our lives. We must have a vision, a dream, and an objective to inspire, direct and motivate us.

Just as it is true that he who expects little will not be disappointed, it is also true that he who expects a lot will not be disappointed. That's why we need to wake up every morning saying, ''Lord, I expect a great deal today. I expect to receive everything Your Word says that I can have, and I expect to be everything You want me to be.''

It is important to have the right attitude, to be enthusiastic and to face each new dawn with the affirmation, **This is the day which the Lord hath made; we will rejoice and be glad in it** (Ps. 118:24). Learn to speak to yourself and to raise your expectations of yourself and what you expect God to do for you.

I expect a lot from God. I expect to be blessed, not because of my natural birth or personal identity, but because of my spiritual birth and divine identity. As a Christian, I am a part of the family of God, I am an heir of God and a joint-heir with Christ. (Rom. 8:17.) If you are a believer, then you are an heir of God and a joint-heir with Christ, too. You have been adopted into the family of God, and you have been made the righteousness of God in Christ. (2 Cor. 5:21.) You and I have a right to expect to be blessed.

I have written this book to help others to see who they are in Christ and to learn how to receive, enjoy and share the abundant, successful and happy life that Jesus Christ has provided for us.

The second quote in Crouch's book that got my attention was, *"If you don't know where you are going, you will probably wind up someplace else."*

This emphasizes our need for a vision, a dream, an objective, a goal. Proverbs 29:18 tells us, **Where there is no vision, the people perish.** Go to God and get His vision. In Habakkuk 2:2,3, the Lord instructed the prophet to write his vision. Likewise, you and I need to make plans — written plans — for our lives.

In Jeremiah 29:11 (NIV), the Lord assures us that He has a plan for each of us, and if we will follow that plan, we will not be disappointed.

> **"For I know the plans I have for you," declares the Lord, "plans to prosper you and not to harm you, plans to give you hope and a future."**

God's plan is to give us peace and success, hope and a future, happiness and achievement, purpose and fulfillment.

In 3 John 2, we read that it is God's desire that we be in health and prosper, even as our soul prospers.

In Psalm 40:1-3, David says that he waited patiently for the Lord and He heard his cry and brought him up out of a horrible pit. David goes on to say that the Lord lifted him up out of the miry clay, set his feet on a rock, established his going and put a new song in his mouth — a song of praise to the Lord.

When you and I accept God's plan for us and we begin to accomplish and fulfill His divine purpose for us, we, too, will be lifted up out of despair and mediocrity and will be set upon a rock. Our mouths will be filled with a new song of praise and thanksgiving to the Lord. We will be easier to get along with. We will treat other people better. We will not only be happier, healthier, and more successful, but we will motivate others to follow the same pattern and receive the same benefits.

Everything in the earth belongs to our heavenly Father Who loves us. Why then should we, His beloved children, live in worry, fear, or anxiety?

In Matthew 6:31-33, Jesus commands us not to worry about what we will eat or drink or wear, because, He says, our heavenly Father knows that we have need of all these things. Instead, He tells us to seek first the Kingdom of God and His righteousness, promising us that if we do so, all the things we need will be added unto us.

In John 10:10, Jesus says that while the enemy comes to steal, kill and destroy, He came that we might have life, and that we might have it more abundantly.

Job 22:23 says that if we will return to the Almighty, we will be edified or built up. Verses 24 and 25 go on to say that we will lay up gold as dust, and that the Lord Himself will be our defense and we will have plenty of silver. That should be reason enough to draw near to the Lord and honor and obey Him.

Finally, Proverbs 13:22 tells us that a good man leaves an inheritance for his children's children, and that the wealth of the sinner is laid up for the just. The ministry of the unrighteous is to toil and accumulate in order to pass their wealth on to the righteous — and in God's time, it will be used to propagate the Good News of Jesus Christ.

In Exodus 3:21,22, the children of Israel were led out of bondage in Egypt, they were told by the Lord to ask their Egyptian owners for all kinds of gold, silver, precious jewels and fine clothing — and it was given to them! The Israelites went out weighted down with goods, because the Bible says that the people of Egypt had been blessed for Joseph's sake. (Gen. 39:5.)

The same is true of God's people today. Wherever we are and whatever we do for a living, those around us will be blessed for our sake.

There is a great transfer of wealth coming. The wealth of the wicked will be placed in the hands of the righteous. But in order for us to be a part of that great transfer of worldly goods, we must first learn to cast our bread upon the waters, confident that if we are faithful and obedient, in a matter of time, it will be returned to us in multiplied form. (Eccl. 11:1.)

God has promised to bless His people abundantly, but if we are to reap that abundance, we must be willing to sow, water, cultivate and harvest — and that takes time and labor. It also takes careful planning.

In His Word, God has promised abundant blessings, but there are 1,056 "ifs" in the Bible. Everything in God's Word is conditional. The Lord has a part to play, and we have a part to play. God always keeps His part of the bargain. The rest is up to you and me.

Whether we reap the benefits depends entirely on whether we are willing to listen, hear, heed and obey the Word of the Lord. That includes the Lord's command to bring the tithe into His storehouse, as we will see in Malachi 3.

Ecclesiastes 2:26 tells us that God gives to those who are good in His sight, wisdom and knowledge and joy. The Bible also says that the steps of a good man — a righteous man — are ordered by the Lord. (Ps. 37:23.)

Psalm 37:18,19 tells us that the Lord knows the days of the upright and that their inheritance will be forever. They will not be ashamed in evil times. Instead of famine, the righteous will enjoy plenty and will be satisfied in time of famine and lack. That is a wonderful promise which should bring reassurance, peace and well-being.

Finally, Psalm 126:5 tells us that those who sow in tears will reap in joy. That's why we must learn to sow our seed in time of famine, of diversity, of hardship.

In these pages, as we examine many passages from the Word of God, I would like to share with you what the Lord has revealed to me about His plan for us to live in happiness, peace, prosperity, health and joy.

To Him be the glory!

Rick Layton

1

God's Way to Prosper

> **For I know the thoughts that I think toward you, saith the Lord, thoughts of peace, and not of evil, to give you an expected end.**
>
> **Jeremiah 29:11**

God has good thoughts, good plans, for His children — thoughts and plans to prosper us and not to harm us. Plans to give us hope and peace and assurance, not despair, worry and anxiety.

This truth is made even more evident in *The Amplified Bible:*

> **For I know the thoughts and plans that I have for you, says the Lord, thoughts and plans for welfare and peace and not for evil, to give you hope in your final outcome.**

The *New American Standard Bible* says:

> **"For I know the plans that I have for you," declares the Lord, "plans for welfare and not for calamity to give you a future and a hope."**

Our Future Is in God

Our future is in God. Like any good parent, He wants His children to be happy, healthy, prosperous and successful. That's one reason I minister on the subject of prosperity and success. I believe that is part of the commission God has given to me. I preach it over and over, because it takes repetition for a word from the Lord to become *rhema.*

Once the revelation becomes imbedded in a person's spirit, he begins to line his life up with it.

Whole new vistas open up to us when we realize that it is the will of God that we prosper and be in health, even as our souls prosper. (3 John 2.) It is uplifting and encouraging to know that God wants us to do the best, have the best, look the best, act the best, think the best, dress the best, talk the best and walk the best.

God wants the best for you and me. If you are living in a shotgun house, He wants you to have a "double-barreled" shotgun house! If you're living in a trailer, He wants you to have a double-wide trailer! God wants you to increase. His plan, dream and vision for you is that you have a hope and a future.

Sowing and Reaping

Be not deceived; God is not mocked: for whatsoever a man soweth, that shall he also reap.
Galatians 6:7

The Apostle Paul tells us that whatever we sow, that is what we will reap. That is as true of the blessings of God as it is for the consequences of sin. If we sow corn, we will harvest corn. If we sow pear seed, we will produce pear trees. If we sow hatred, we will reap hatred. If we sow love, we will reap love.

In agricultural terms, we understand the principle that what we plant in the form of seed will produce the same kind of fruit. Yet when it comes to the Kingdom of God, some people have the mistaken idea that they can reap what they have never sown — or avoid reaping what they have sown. It just doesn't work that way.

One of the reasons God wants us to be blessed is so we can be a blessing to others. No one can give what he does not have. If we are to bless other people, we must first be blessed. No one can draw out of an account in which he has deposited nothing.

The Way to Prosper

> **For he that soweth to his flesh shall of the flesh reap corruption; but he that soweth to the Spirit shall of the Spirit reap life everlasting.**
>
> **And let us not be weary in well-doing: for in due season we shall reap, if we faint not.**
>
> **Galatians 6:8,9**

Your harvest is coming. You will reap if you faint not. What you reap in the future will depend on what you are sowing now.

If you are in a dilemma right now, or if you are facing hardship and famine, begin to sow. As you increase your sowing, your harvest will also increase.

That means going beyond the tithe. As we will see in a later chapter, tithing is not giving to the Lord; it is returning to God that which is already His. Tithing is our reasonable service. It is only when we go beyond the tithe that we begin to give "offerings" unto the Lord.

Willing and Obedient

> **If ye be willing and obedient, ye shall eat the good of the land.**
>
> **Isaiah 1:19**

If this verse is true, and Scripture says God cannot lie, then it must also be true that if we are *not* willing and obedient, we will *not* eat the good of the land. When we disobey God in any area of life, we bring a curse upon ourselves and we open the door of our lives to the work of the enemy. When we do what is right, God will intervene and rebuke the devourer for our sakes. (Mal. 3:11.)

There are times when we won't be able to see what the devil is doing. He may be working while we are asleep. But the good news is, God never slumbers nor sleeps. (Ps. 121:4.) He watches over His Word to perform it on our behalf as we put our trust in Him. (Jer. 1:12.) Even while we are at rest, the Lord shields, protects and stops the enemy in his tracks.

God's Promise

> **Bring ye all the tithes into the storehouse, that there may be meat in mine house, and prove me now herewith, saith the Lord of hosts, if I will not open you the windows of heaven, and pour you out a blessing, that there shall not be room enough to receive it.**
>
> **And I will rebuke the devourer for your sakes....**
>
> **Malachi 3:10,11**

There are many ways the Lord can keep you from being "devoured" by the enemy. It may be something as simple as showing you a rock in your yard so the lawn mower isn't damaged or broken. It may be quickening you that it is time to change the oil in your car so it doesn't get clogged up and burn out the engine.

The Lord says that His sheep hear His voice and follow Him, but *a stranger they will not follow.* (John 10:5.) Obedient sheep hear the voice of the Good Shepherd. They walk with Him and are kept by Him in all their ways.

As Christians, we walk not after the flesh, but after the Spirit. (Rom. 8:4.) There is nothing Satan can do to a born-again child of God without the Lord warning him in advance of the plans, devices and schemes of the enemy. If you and I walk with the Lord, we will always be forewarned of the devil's schemes and plots.

That is reason enough to be willing and obedient, to tithe and give offerings to the Lord.

If we will learn to be willing and obedient, to give the Lord His tithe, to seek first His Kingdom and His righteousness, then we are assured of receiving all those things that we need, just as God promised in His Word.

Sometimes that principle is hard for us to get hold of, especially when we have a long history of robbing God by not bringing into His house all the tithes. The Lord commands us to bring in the full tithe so that there can be meat and provision in His house. When there is meat and provision in the house of the Lord, we will have what we need to evangelize the whole world. We will be able to afford radio and television time to reach millions who need to hear the Gospel.

If everyone in the Church of Jesus Christ would begin to tithe their income, we could reach the world for the Lord in a very short time.

Yet, some people think that to preach the blessing of God upon the tithe is to preach the law. One minister I once knew would take me into a back room of the church and lecture me about preaching law rather than grace. He would even give me books on this subject. He was convinced that I was wrong in what I was preaching. I finally told him, "You have reached me too late. I believe that God does bless those who are willing and obedient."

He would get mad and storm off. There was a spirit of rebellion in him. Every time I ministered on the subject of prosperity and success, he reacted negatively. Yet, I only preached what I read in the Word of God. I preached that whatever a person sows, that is what he will reap.

I Wish Above All Things

Beloved, I wish above all things that thou mayest prosper and be in health, even as thy soul prospereth.
3 John 2

Sometimes we Christians — especially we black believers — think that to serve God we must be big. We must have big churches and big ministries. God is not against bigness, but that is not always a sign of His blessing or favor. People don't care what size church you have as long as they know that you are preaching and living the Word of God. If a person preaches and lives the Word of God, he will prosper simply because God said he would.

The Word of God brings wisdom, and wisdom produces wealth. But in order for believers to receive and enjoy the riches that the Lord wants to bestow upon us, we must learn to be willing and obedient. It takes all of us working together to fulfill the vision that God has given us as individuals and as a church.

God has said that it is His desire for us to prosper and be in good health. It is His plan for us that we have hope and a future, an expected end.

This is God's plan and will, His dream and vision for you and me. He says that He desires this "above all things." More than anything else, God wills that His children be prosperous and in good health.

God doesn't want us to be sick in our bodies. He wants us to be whole. His plan is to heal us so we can walk in divine health. When we are sick, we cannot work with Him as productively as He desires. We become part of the problem instead of part of the solution.

Faith Is Not Foolishness

But if any provide not for his own, and specially

> **for those of his own house, he hath denied the faith, and is worse than an infidel.**
>
> **1 Timothy 5:8**

God wants us healthy, wealthy and wise. He wants us to have more than enough to take care of ourselves and our families so we are in a position to bless others.

In His Word, God says that a person who will not take care of His own family is worse than an infidel, one who has denied the faith. This is worse than being an unbeliever. If you and I will not take care of our families, then we are not pleasing to God.

It has never been God's will for His children to use "faith" as an excuse not to work and provide an honest living for themselves and those who depend upon them.

It is true that we are to live by faith (Rom. 1:17), but living by faith is not quitting a job and relying on somcone else to support you. Living by faith is not throwing away money on get-rich-quick schemes. Living by faith is not depending on the government or the church to feed, clothe and house you. Living by faith is being honest in your dealings with others, with yourself and with the Lord.

Remember the Lord Thy God

> **And thou say in thine heart, My power and the might of mine hand hath gotten me this wealth.**
>
> **But thou shalt remember the Lord thy God: for it is he that giveth thee power to get wealth, that he may establish his covenant which he sware unto thy fathers, as it is this day.**
>
> **Deuteronomy 8:17,18**

Some Christians think that because they are required to provide for themselves and their families, both the wife and the husband have to work. I believe it is the Lord's will that the mother stay home and take care of the children while they are small. My wife worked for a time after we were married, but later she quit her job to be home with the children.

Sometimes we get the idea that because we Christians are told to work with our own hands (1 Thess. 4:11), that means everyone in the household is to be employed. We look at the current economic situation and think that both parents have to be out in the work force to be able to make it.

But the Lord says that it is not by our power or might that we get wealth, but He gives it to us. One reason it may be taking two, three, four, or more in your family just to make ends meet is because you are not willing and obedient to the Lord in the area of your finances.

Remember, it is not your talent, ability, or drive that brings in the wealth. It is God's intervention in your situation, giving you favor with those in authority over you on the job, getting you that raise or promotion. God works with those who trust and rely on Him, those who put their confidence not in their own human ability but in His divine ability.

God wants to prosper you so you can fulfill your dream, vision and plan — that which He has placed in your heart. For some, that may take ten thousand dollars. For others, it may take a million. Whatever your goal or desire, commit it to the Lord and allow Him to show you how to fulfill it.

Why does the Lord give you power to get wealth, to be prosperous, to be successful? So He can establish His covenant in the earth. God's blessings are not for us to hoard up in banks and vaults, but they are given to us to accomplish His plan and spread His Gospel throughout the earth.

If you will devote yourself to that purpose, you *will* be blessed and you *will* prosper — God's way.

2
Tithes and Offerings

Will You Rob Me?

Will a man rob God? Yet ye have robbed me. But ye say, Wherein have we robbed thee? In tithes and offerings.

Ye are cursed with a curse: for ye have robbed me, even this whole nation.

Malachi 3:8,9

Through the prophet, Malachi, the Lord asks His people, ''Will you rob Me?'' What does He mean? You can rob God by withholding your tithes — a tenth of *everything* the Lord provides for you.

Tithing is not an option. It is a command. It is evidence of honesty. Only honest people tithe. Remember, you and I are not being generous when we tithe. We are just doing our duty. We are simply returning God's portion to Him. When we tithe, we do nothing worthy of praise. The tithe belongs to God, not to us. When we give Him a tenth of all our income, we are doing our reasonable service. We have nothing to boast about just because we pay our debts — to God or to man. That is the least that is expected of an honest person.

That's why the Lord set up the tithe system — to find out how honest a man or woman is. The tithe is evidence of integrity. If a person is honest, he has no choice but to be a tither. Show me an individual who has not committed to tithe, and I will show you a person who is dishonest in other areas of his life.

If God has to struggle and wrestle with an individual to get from him what is rightfully His, then you can be sure that other people have to do the same.

The only reason many people do not tithe is because they have never been taught to do so. In a sense, we can't hold others responsible for what they have never been taught. But after they have heard the Word of the Lord about the tithe, once they understand that the first tenth belongs to the Lord and that to withhold it is to rob God, then they are accountable and responsible for their actions.

If a person will steal from God, he will steal from others. An individual who refuses to tithe, to return to the Lord what is rightfully His, is an individual who loves money. There is nothing wrong with money or with being financially prosperous. As we have seen, God wants His children to prosper and do well. The problem is in loving money, in putting it ahead of God. That is what is meant when the Bible says in 1 Timothy 6:10 (NIV), **the love of money is a root of all kinds of evil.** What greater evil could there be than robbing God?

Learn to Communicate

> **Let him that is taught in the word communicate unto him that teacheth in all good things.**
>
> **Galatians 6:6**

*The Amplified Translation*of this verse reads:

> **Let him who receives instruction in the Word** [of God] **share all good things with his teacher** [contributing to his support].

As we have seen, the only way for the child of God to prosper is God's way. That's why when people tell me they can't afford to tithe, I tell them I can't afford *not* to tithe. When you are in bad financial shape or when you have nothing, you have nothing to lose. Since your way hasn't worked, why not give up and do it God's way?

Some people claim that they don't tithe or give to the Church because all preachers want is their money. That is not so. God doesn't call and establish people in the ministry to get money out of other people. Preachers are not God's tax collectors. They are His servants, His representatives, His spokesmen. He has set them in the Church to preach His Word so others will be blessed and prospered — in every aspect of life. They should be supported because by doing the work of the Lord, they are blessing many people.

It is right to support the man or woman of God. The world is not going to do it, because it's not their responsibility. The Church of Jesus Christ belongs to God and to His people, not to the world. The Church is God's system, not the devil's. And if we are a part of that system, then we need to support it in every way possible. Why? We will be the ones who reap the benefits from it.

If we expect to benefit from the work of the Lord, then we should build and sustain that work. We should be willing and obedient to share all good things with our teachers — contributing to their support. That is sowing into the Kingdom of God. That is doing it God's way. And it *will* be rewarded. We *will* reap what we sow. God has guaranteed it.

Put God First

But seek ye first the kingdom of God, and his

righteousness; and all these things shall be added unto you.

Matthew 6:33

To be prosperous, we must put God first. He has clearly promised that when we put Him first, He will add unto us everything that we need.

I get upset when I hear people complain about the prosperity message. The ones who complain are usually the very ones who aren't giving. Often, it is because they have nothing to give. The reason they have nothing to give today is because they have given nothing in the past.

They want to receive from the Lord, but they don't know how. Many of them don't know or believe that God wants them to be blessed, prosperous and successful. They don't seem to realize that just as they want their own children to be healthy, wealthy and wise, God wants the same for His children.

Sometimes such people are jealous or envious when others are blessed by the Lord. That attitude also robs them of blessings. It is impossible to receive from the Lord what we begrudge in others. Just as withholding the tithe from the Lord keeps us from receiving from Him, when we deny God's blessings to others, we cut off the very channel that He wants to use to direct His blessings to us.

One reason we black people are so rude sometimes is because we have nothing. We resent the fact that others — especially white people — are so much more prosperous than we are. We have no businesses, no jobs, nothing to give to society. I believe that God is changing that situation in our day. He is raising up a new breed of people, a breed of black Cushites, who will have something to give to their brothers and sisters — black, white, red and yellow.

But in order for that vision to come to pass, we must learn to give so that we can receive. We must learn to rejoice in the blessings of others, so that we may share in it.

Our black churches should be so prosperous that we can afford to hire staff members to help us do the work of the Lord, not only in our own areas but around the world. We need to learn to support our ministers, those who labor among us in the fields of the Lord.

God has a plan and purpose for each of us, but if we are to carry out that plan and fulfill that purpose, we need to walk in His Word and put Him first. We can't expect to reap what we have not sown. In order to reap, we must learn to give tithes and offerings.

Be Faithful Stewards

> **He that is faithful in that which is least is faithful also in much: and he that is unjust in the least is unjust also in much.**
>
> **If therefore ye have not been faithful in the unrighteous mammon, who will commit to your trust the true riches?**
>
> **And if we have not been faithful in that which is another man's, who shall give you that which is your own?**
>
> **Luke 16:10-12**

Each of us wants God to bless us. We want Him to set us into positions of authority and power in the Church and in the world. But He cannot do that for us if we do not live up to the standards demanded of those who fill such high positions of trust and responsibility.

That's why the Lord taught the principle that he who is faithful in little will be faithful also in much. That includes returning to the Lord what is His.

In our church, we have a rule that no one can be in a leadership position if he does not tithe, because the tithe shows where that individual's heart is. The tithe is the test of each believer's honesty and integrity. If a person is not honest with God, then we feel that he cannot be trusted to exercise authority or leadership over others.

A person who tithes shows that he is willing to communicate with others, as we saw in Galatians 6:6. Such a person has a giving spirit. He is willing to give — whether it is money or love. He is a good steward of God's blessings. He is faithful in that which is little. He is careful how he lives before others. He doesn't defile the temple of the Lord, which is his own body. He knows that it is not enough just to tithe; he must also be faithful in every other area of life.

A believer can tithe until his tongue hangs out, but if he doesn't live right, then he will not receive the greater blessings of the Lord. In sowing and reaping, attitude is as important as action.

It is also important to be a good steward of what the Lord has already entrusted to your care. If you won't take care of a bicycle, then you can't be trusted with a motorcycle. If you are believing God for a new car, then take care of the old one you already own. Even if you have to drive it until the wheels fall off, when the wrecker comes to tow it away, the mechanic should say, "That is the cleanest, best-looking pile of junk I ever saw!" That's being a good steward of God's possessions.

Be faithful in the little, and God will bless you with much.

There is no need to talk about making a hundred thousand dollars a year if you won't tithe off the ten thousand you are making now. When you get a hundred thousand, you will just be stealing on a larger scale. The reason you aren't getting a hundred thousand is because God knows you can't be trusted. You have proven it by your actions in handling the little that He has already given you.

God does not bless selfishness or reward dishonesty.

Bring In All the Tithe

Bring ye all the tithes into the storehouse, that there may be meat in mine house, and prove me now herewith, saith the Lord of hosts, if I will not open you the windows of heaven, and pour you out a blessing, that there shall not be room enough to receive it.

And I will rebuke the devourer for your sakes, and he shall not destroy the fruits of your ground; neither shall your vine cast her fruit before the time in the field, saith the Lord of hosts.

And all nations shall call you blessed: for ye shall be a delightsome land, saith the Lord of hosts.

Malachi 3:10-12

In these verses, the Lord makes it plain that tithing is not optional. It is a commandment from God. It is not up to us to decide whether we would like to tithe or not. The only option we have is *how much* we will *give beyond the tithe* — how much offering we will give to the Lord.

The offering is optional. By the amount of offering we give, we determine the amount of blessing we will receive in return. But the tithe itself is not negotiable.

The Offerings

But this I say, He which soweth sparingly shall reap also sparingly; and he which soweth bountifully shall reap also bountifully.

Every man according as he purposeth in his heart, so let him give; not grudgingly, or of necessity: for God loveth a cheerful giver.

2 Corinthians 9:6,7

Although the Lord has assured His people that they will be rewarded for their willingness and obedience in bringing in the tithes, we are not given the option of deciding what is to be done with that tithe. It is with the offering that we do have *some say* in deciding where it goes and for what purpose.

When you give an offering, when you give to a church fund or donate to a ministry — every time you sow your gifts into a particular work — you should specify to God what you want in return. When you give your gifts and offerings, let Him know what you are sowing for.

The principle is: The tithe gets God to the window, and the offering opens the window. Before the offering can become respectable, there must be the tithe.

We must approach God His way — and His way is, first the tithe, then the offering. The larger the offering, the larger the blessing. The greater the offering, the wider the window.

That's why this passage says that every man should give as he purposes in his own heart. The tithe is not purposed by the one who gives it; it is purposed by the Lord. The tithe belongs to God; there is no deciding one way or the other about it. God has already set the boundaries on that subject. The tithe comes first, off the top — the gross, not the net. Once that obligation is met, then the person can purpose or decide in his heart *how much* he wants to *give* in the offering.

According to the Bible, every person is supposed to give his offerings to the Lord out of a sense of willingness, not of necessity. Each of us must decide how much we *want* to give in offerings — and therefore how much we *want* to be blessed. That is a step of faith.

So many people have misunderstood God's financial system. They think that they decide how much to give God out of *the total amount* they have received from Him. That is not so. It is only *after* the tithe is made that the deciding is done.

Once the amount of the offering has been determined, it must be given willingly and cheerfully. God loves a cheerful, happy giver. When you plant, you should be full of joy.

God's Way

> **And God is able to make all grace abound toward you; that ye, always having all sufficiency in all things, may abound to every good work.**
>
> **2 Corinthians 9:8**

The tithe gets the seed into the ground. The offering waters the seed. Without water, there is no growth.

That's why God told the people that they were under a curse, because they were robbing Him. When they asked Him, "How have we robbed You?" He answered, "In tithes and offerings." Yet, He never designated how much those offerings should be. But we can see clearly how much the tithe is — its very name means a tenth.

When we render to the Lord the tithe — the tenth of all our income, that which is rightfully His — followed up with our own *freewill* offerings, then we can expect to be blessed, to have all sufficiency in all things so that we may abound to every good work.

That is God's plan, His system for prosperity and success.

3
Sow For It!

> **Now he that ministereth seed to the sower both minister bread for your food, and multiply your seed sown, and increase the fruits of your righteousness;**
>
> **Being enriched in every thing to all bountifulness, which causeth through us thanksgiving to God.**
>
> **2 Corinthians 9:10,11**

The *New American Standard Version* of this passage reads:

> **Now He who supplies seed to the sower and bread for food, will supply and multiply your seed for sowing and increase the harvest of your righteousness;**
>
> **You will be enriched in everything for all liberality, which through us is producing thanksgiving to God.**

The Apostle Paul makes it clear that when we sow seed into the work of the Lord, He has promised to multiply that seed back to us. He will increase the harvest our seed produces so that we will be made rich in every way, making it possible for us to give generously to every good work.

Sow to Reap

> **For unto every one that hath shall be given, and he shall have abundance: but from him that hath not**

shall be taken away even that which he hath.
Matthew 25:29

If you need a job, what do you do? You sow for it. If you need a new automobile, what do you do? You sow for it. If you need a new home, what do you do? You sow for it. Whatever you need in life, sow for it! If a person will not sow, God cannot provide seed for that individual.

The Apostle Paul says that God provides seed for the sower. That means that each of us has something that we can sow — some kind of seed that we can invest in the work of the Lord. As we sow what we have, then the Lord increases that seed — and thus our harvest — so that we have even more to invest. As we see in the parable of the talents told by Jesus, the one who takes his Master's seed and invests it wisely will be given even more; but the one who holds on to what he has been given will lose even that.

Our return is determined, not just by how much we sow, but by the attitude in which we sow it. As we saw in verses 7 and 8 of 2 Corinthians 9, the Lord loves a cheerful giver, one who gives willingly and not out of a sense of obligation or necessity.

We should be glad when we have an opportunity to sow into the Lord's work. If we give anything to someone in need, we can do it cheerfully, knowing that we will receive our reward.

Some people wonder why they keep giving, yet never seem to get anything in return. Sometimes it is because of their "stinking thinking." If the attitude is wrong, the giving is in vain. A wrong attitude closes the windows of heaven and blocks the outpouring of blessing that God wants to bestow upon the sower, the giver.

In order to hear from God, to receive from the Lord, we must keep the channels of communication open between Him and us and between our neighbor and ourselves. We do that by keeping our hearts right before the Lord and our relationships with others in accordance with His will.

One time my wife and I wanted to go out to eat, but we didn't have enough money to pay for a meal. I had sowed all that I had on me, so there was nothing left. At that moment, a dear sister came by the office and said, "I just feel like God told me to bring you this." It was a gift of money. As a result, we were able to eat a nice meal and rejoice in the Lord.

The reason that lady did that was because she had the right attitude toward us and toward the Lord. She knew how to sow cheerfully and to reap bountifully.

God can never speak to us to give anything of any significance if we are tight and stingy, or if we have an attitude that resents giving to others. God knows that we cannot sow what we do not have. He has told us that we are to give what we have, not what we don't have. Too often the problem is that we have it to give, but we don't want to part with it. Without a right attitude, our giving will profit us nothing.

Sow As the Lord Directs

> **Give, and it shall be given unto you; good measure, pressed down, and shaken together, and running over, shall men give into your bosom. For with the same measure that ye mete withal it shall be measured to you again.**
>
> **Luke 6:38**

God does not expect or direct us to sow into every good work. He will tell us where we are to invest that which He has bestowed upon us.

God has never led me to sow into everything. I can watch good Christian television programs, yet not send any money to them. But if I watch some on a regular basis, then the Lord moves me to become a part in their ministry.

The same should be true of you. If you receive a blessing from a certain program, church, or ministry, then you should support that work financially. Don't be stingy, and don't associate with stingy people — those who want to receive but never give. Everyone wants to be blessed, but some people don't want to be a blessing. That is not God's way to prosper.

If you will do God's will, He has promised to take care of you, and God cannot lie. (Num. 23:19.)

Some people like to quote scriptures that seem to say that God will bless everyone, no matter what they do or don't do. They will quote the passage that says that God causes the rain to fall on the just and on the unjust alike. (Matt. 5:45.) It is true that God is good to all, but it is also true that He reserves His richest blessings for those who are pleasing to Him, those who are partners with Him in His work.

I believe God obligates Himself to the person who does His Word.

Sow With the Right Attitude

Sometimes people come into my office and say, "Pastor, I'm tithing and giving, I'm sowing into the Lord's work. But I am still hurting, still in need. What's wrong?"

I will say to them, "I suggest you look back over your life and check. Something is missing. It may be just an attitude problem. But you are doing something that is keeping you from receiving God's best."

You can give a thousand dollars to the church and not get blessed as much as you should. Although it is true that if you give, it will be given back to you in good measure, that what you sow you will reap, it is also true that what you give must be given cheerfully and willingly and with the right attitude of heart.

Sow For a Purpose

> **. . . So is the kingdom of God, as if a man should cast seed into the ground;**
>
> **And should sleep, and rise night and day, and the seed should spring and grow up, he knoweth not how.**
>
> **For the earth bringeth forth fruit of herself; first the blade, then the ear, after that the full corn in the ear.**
>
> **But when the fruit is brought forth, immediately he putteth in the sickle, because the harvest is come.**
>
> **Mark 4:26-29**

When I sow my seed, I label it. No farmer goes out and puts just any kind of seed into the ground. If he wants cotton, he plants cotton. If he wants wheat, he sows wheat. If he wants corn, he plants corn.

Without a name, the seed does not know what to produce. So when I sow, I say, "Lord, I am sowing new car seed." Then I don't start worrying how that seed is going to germinate and grow and produce fruit. I just go on my way, praising and thanking the Lord, trusting that He will see that the seed reproduces exactly what I have sown.

That's what you should do.

Perhaps you have been sowing seed, then wondering and worrying how you are going to cause it to grow and produce what you want. The Lord said He will take care of that. Your job is to sow. His job is to water. He does that with the words that come out of your mouth.

When you sow your seed, have a purpose. Know what you are sowing that seed for. Not only will you harvest *what* you have sown, but you will also harvest *in proportion* to the amount you have sown. If you sow little, you will reap little. If you sow much, you will reap much.

Don't be afraid to give God your best — and then expect His best in return. If the Lord can't trust you to tithe a hundred dollars, then you will never get a thousand. You must be faithful in the little you have if you are to be trusted to handle the much that He desires to pour out upon you.

I remember when I could only give thirty cents a week to the work of the Lord. I also remember the times when I could give as much as thirteen hundred dollars in tithes — besides my gifts. No matter what the size of my gift, it is the Lord who gives me the power to get wealth. I also know that when I do what is right, God blesses me through all kinds of sources.

The Lord is true to His Word. I know because I have proven Him — over and over. And what He has done for me, He will do for you — if you will sow into His work in faith.

Sow in Faith

Therefore it is of faith, that it might be by grace; to the end the promise might be sure to all the seed; not to that only which is of the law, but to that also which is of the faith of Abraham; who is the father of us all,

(As it is written, I have made thee a father of many nations,) before him whom he believed, even

God, who quickeneth the dead, and calleth those things which be not as though they were.

Romans 4:16,17

If you want to prosper in any area of life, you must have the faith of Abraham. You must have absolute confidence in God. You must learn to do as He did and call those things that be not as though they already were.

You must learn to speak that thing you desire into existence. After you have spoken, then you must begin to act as if what you have spoken is so. For example, if you are believing God for a raise, start acting as if you already have that raise. Start tithing on that amount.

Hope Against Hope

Who against hope believed in hope, that he might become the father of many nations, according to that which was spoken, So shall thy seed be.

Romans 4:18

God told Abraham, "I have made you the father of many nations." At that time, Abraham did not have a son, and he was far too old to produce an offspring with his wife, Sarah, who was barren. Yet, the Bible tells us that Abraham against hope believed in hope.

Despite the outward circumstances, Abraham had faith. He believed that what God had said about him would come to pass just as He had promised.

In your situation, it may appear that things are impossible. It may look as if you will never get a job, a raise, a nicer home, or a newer car. That's why you must get the Word of the Lord for your situation and then do as faithful Abraham and believe God — regardless of the way things may appear.

Look Not at Things That Are Seen

While we look not at the things which are seen, but at the things which are not seen: for the things which are seen are temporal; but the things which are not seen are eternal.

2 Corinthians 4:18

The Word that Abraham received was spoken directly to him by God. In order for you to have the faith of Abraham, you must hear from the Lord for yourself. Go to His Word and find the scriptures that deal with your particular need or situation. Get several translations of the Bible so you can meditate on these passages. Write them down, believe them wholeheartedly, which is standing on them and quote them daily. Call those things that be not as though they were.

That's what I did when we needed a new building. I stood on the grounds and spoke forth my faith day after day until I saw that building actually become a physical reality. Whatever it is that you are seeking from the Lord, whether it is financial prosperity, physical healing, or spiritual renewal, after you have sown your seed, stand on His Word of promise until you receive.

Thank the Lord for what He has given you, even before it materializes. When Satan comes to tempt you to doubt, stand against him in faith, refusing to listen to him because he is a liar, and the father of liars. (John 8:44.)

God Does Not Lie

God is not a man, that he should lie; neither the son of man, that he should repent: hath he said, and shall he not do it? or hath he spoken, and shall he not make it good?

Numbers 23:19

God's blessings, like prosperity and success, are not the result of wishing but of believing. They do not come by chance but by choice. That choice is Jesus Christ and the Word of God.

No matter how things may appear to be or what people may say about you, act on the Word of the Lord. Remember that what you see is temporal, temporary, subject to change. Stand on the Word of the Lord until you see what you have desired manifested.

If you are living right, you will prosper and be blessed. God has given you His Word, and He cannot lie.

4
Destroying the Root of Debt

Thou shalt truly tithe all the increase of thy seed, that the field bringeth forth year by year.
Deuteronomy 14:22

As the Church of the Lord Jesus Christ, we need to destroy the root of debt. We need to be set free financially so that we can establish the covenant of God, as He has commanded. If all of God's people were out of debt, think what we could do for His Kingdom on earth!

I believe the Church of Jesus Christ is going to become the debt-free Church of the nineties. I believe that is God's will for this generation. But there is only one way that this vision can come to pass and that is for God's people to begin to obey the Word of the Lord in regard to their material possessions.

When we serve the Lord, He has promised to take care of us, that is true. But, as we have seen, there is a part that we play in having our needs met. One of the things we are to do is to free ourselves from debt. We begin that process by paying, first of all, what we owe the Lord.

The Firstfruits

The first of the firstfruits of thy land thou shalt bring into the house of the Lord thy God....
Exodus 23:19

As we have seen, the tithe belongs to the Lord. We are commanded to set aside and bring to Him a tenth of everything we receive. But this is not just any tenth, it is what the Bible calls the *firstfruits* — the first and best of all our increase.

The *increase* means the gross amount we receive, not the net. We tithe off the entire sum of our income, not what we have left over after paying what we owe others, like the government. That is our obligation, our debt to the Lord, And we cannot expect to prosper if we do not meet this primary responsibility and duty.

The Tithe Is Holy

And all of the tithe of the land, whether of the seed of the land, or of the fruit of the tree, is the Lord's: it is holy unto the Lord.

Leviticus 27:30

The tithe is holy unto the Lord. It is that amount of what He has provided for us that He reserves for Himself and His work. To hold back that portion for our own personal use is to rob God. No one who robs the Lord can ever hope to be blessed by Him.

That means that of any income we receive beyond the expenses of producing that income, the first 10 percent belongs to the Lord and must be paid to Him before any other bills are paid.

For example, if I bought a car for a thousand dollars and sold it for the same price, I would owe the Lord nothing because there was no increase, no profit. However, if I sold that car for eleven hundred dollars, then I would make a hundred dollars profit, of which 10 percent, or ten dollars, would be the Lord's rightful share.

That is fair, because no one ever has to match someone else's giving. Each of us — whether we are on a fixed income like Social Security or whether we are a millionaire making hundreds of thousands of dollars a year — pays the same percentage, one tenth. That means that we don't have to worry about how much anyone else is giving because we can know that he is giving the same as we are, one tenth.

That also means that we cannot say that we can't afford to tithe, because all God asks of us is the first tenth of whatever He blesses us with. If we have no blessing — if there is no increase, no income — then we have no obligation. If our income is small, then our tithe is small. As our income grows, the part we owe the Lord also grows in direct proportion. So it is not true that some of us can't tithe. Every one can, and God has commanded us to do so.

The only way to get out of debt to others is to get out of debt to the Lord. Do you want to be debt free? Then start tithing.

Thou Shalt Bring the Tithe

> **And it shall be, when thou art come in unto the land which the Lord thy God giveth thee for an inheritance, and possessest it, and dwellest therein;**
>
> **That thou shalt take of the first of all the fruit of the earth, which thou shalt bring of thy land that the Lord thy God giveth thee, and shalt put it in a basket, and shalt go unto the place which the Lord thy God shall choose to place his name there.**
>
> **And thou shalt go unto the priest that shall be in those days, and say unto him....**
>
> **...Behold, I have brought the firstfruits of the land, which thou, O Lord, hast given me. And thou shalt set it before the Lord thy God, and worship before the Lord thy God.**
>
> **Deuteronomy 26:1-3,10**

Some people say that all we preachers talk about is money, about tithes and offerings. The reason we talk so much about these things is because God talks so much about them in His Word. If we preach the Word, we must preach about money.

Another reason we talk so much about these things is because we know that the only way anyone can be blessed and prosper and live free of debt is by obeying the commands of the Lord. And the Lord has commanded that His people bring their tithes to Him, and worship Him with them. This is not an option for the New Testament believer any more than it was for the Old Testament Hebrew.

Honor the Lord With Your Firstfruits

> **Honour the Lord with thy substance, and with the firstfruits of all thine increase:**
>
> **So shall thy barns be filled with plenty, and thy presses shall burst out with new wine.**
>
> **Proverbs 3:9,10**

The Lord has promised that if we will do as He commands and worship and honor Him by bringing to Him our tithes, the firstfruits of all our increase, then He will see to it that our barns are filled with plenty and our presses burst out with new wine.

In modern language, we might say that our checking accounts will be full and our savings accounts will be overflowing. Another way to look at this promise is that we will have a fresh anointing. Our lives will be filled with the new wine of God's Holy Spirit. If we will be obedient to the Lord's commands with our material goods, we will reap manifold blessings, both materially and spiritually.

Abraham Was a Tither

> **And Melchizedek king of Salem brought forth bread and wine: and he was the priest of the most high God.**

And he blessed him, and said, Blessed be Abram of the most high God, possessor of heaven and earth:

And blessed be the most high God, which hath delivered thine enemies into thy hand. And he gave him tithes of all.

Genesis 14:18-20

Some Christians, especially some blacks in the Church, know nothing about tithes and offerings. They have never been taught the principles of sowing and reaping. That's one reason some black believers are not as prosperous as many of their white brothers and sisters. They have an aversion to money sermons. As soon as the minister begins to talk on this subject, they start squirming. They think that all he is after is their pocketbook. Some will even leave a church before they will pay their tithe or make a pledge. That's why I preach this message so much, so that believers — both black and white — will learn how to prosper God's way. And God's way is to tithe.

Even faithful Abraham was a tither. When he met Melchizedek, after coming back from recovering his stolen goods from a foreign king, he freely gave a tenth of everything to the Lord's high priest. As a result, Abraham received a blessing from the priest and became even more wealthy than before. The more he gave, the more he received. That is the lesson our people must learn if they are ever to live as God intends.

Jacob Was a Tither

And Jacob vowed a vow, saying, If God will be with me, and will keep me in this way that I go, and will give me bread to eat, and raiment to put on,

So that I come again to my father's house in peace; then shall the Lord be my God:

> **And this stone, which I have set for a pillar, shall be God's house: and of all that thou shalt give me I will surely give the tenth unto thee.**
>
> **Genesis 28:20-22**

Abraham did not tithe because he was a born-again believer, and neither did Jacob. Even though they were not born again, the Lord blessed them beyond measure so that they became extremely wealthy men. If Abraham and Jacob did not live in debt, then neither should God's people today.

Why shouldn't we be debt free? We should be, and we can be if we will simply do as God commands and be faithful, just as Abraham and Jacob were.

The Lord has promised again and again to bless everything that we put our hands to and to increase us in goods — just as He did Abraham and Jacob — if we will walk in His ways and be obedient to His commands.

Obedience Produces Plenty

> **Moreover he commanded the people that dwelt in Jerusalem to give the portion of the priests and the Levites, that they might be encouraged in the law of the Lord.**
>
> **And as soon as the commandment came abroad, the children of Israel brought in abundance the firstfruits of corn, wine, and oil, and honey, and of all the increase of the field; and the tithe of all things brought they in abundantly.**
>
> **2 Chronicles 31:4,5**

As a result of their obedience to the command of the Lord to bring the firstfruits to the priests and Levites, the people were blessed so that the chief priest could declare:

> **. . . Since the people began to bring the offerings into the house of the Lord we have had enough to eat,**

and have left plenty: for the Lord hath blessed his people; and that which is left is this great store.
2 Chronicles 31:10

When the Lord's people were obedient to His command, He multiplied their gifts so that they all had plenty to eat and a great deal left over. They did not live in debt, and neither should God's people live in debt today.

Launch Out Into the Deep

Now when he had left speaking, he said unto Simon, Launch out into the deep, and let down your nets for a draught.

And Simon answering said unto him, Master, we have toiled all the night, and have taken nothing: nevertheless at thy word I will let down the net.

And when they had this done, they enclosed a great multitude of fishes: and their net brake.

And they beckoned unto their partners, which were in the other ship, that they should come and help them. And they came, and filled both the ships, so that they began to sink.
Luke 5:4-7

The only reason some people don't tithe is because of fear. They're afraid that if they give to the Lord what is due Him, they won't have enough to meet their own needs. It doesn't seem to make sense to give away what you need yourself — especially when you don't even have enough as it is. That's why this message about sowing and reaping has to be preached, so that people can understand that *it is their very giving that produces their return.*

This is also why this message has to be received by spiritual ears — because it doesn't make sense to the natural or carnal mind.

The reason many of God's people — especially many black believers — haven't been blessed abundantly is because they have been holding back the tithe. It is impossible to be blessed abundantly while robbing God. Such people must learn to launch out into the deep — by faith. That means giving *before* receiving. Tithing means trusting God to return much more than what was given.

Simon Peter and his brother, Andrew, obeyed the Lord's command, even though they knew there were no fish in the sea because they had been fishing there all night. Yet, when they did as they were told and let down their net, they received such an abundance that they had to call their partners to come help them. They hauled in so many fish that their ships began to sink. That is an abundant return!

Just as Peter obeyed the Lord, even though it seemed hopeless and a waste, we must learn to obey the Lord and give out of our need. When we do, He has promised to return to us what we have given in multiplied form — good measure, pressed down, shaken together and overflowing!

Return Unto the Lord

> **Even from the days of your fathers ye are gone away from mine ordinances, and have not kept them. Return unto me, and I will return unto you, saith the Lord of hosts....**
>
> **Malachi 3:7**

In this passage, the Lord tells us that although we have not been keeping His commandments, if we will return to Him, then He will return to us. How do we do that? What does the Lord want us to return to Him?

Immediately after this verse, the Lord asks the question, **Will a man rob God?** (v. 8.) When asked by

His people how they have been robbing Him, He answers, **In** [your] **tithes and offerings.**

In other words, the way we return to God is by returning to Him the firstfruits, the tithe — the first tenth of what He has given us.

Notice the promise that goes with this commandment. If we will return to the Lord, He will return to us. If we will be faithful with the unrighteous mammon, our money, then He will entrust to us the true riches, His blessings. (Luke 16:11.)

He even goes on to say that we are under a curse when we fail to return to Him what is His. (Mal. 3:9.) He exhorts us to put Him to the test by our tithes, assuring us that if we will do so, He will open to us the windows of heaven and pour out upon us such a blessing that there will not be room enough to contain it. (v. 10.)

He also promises that He will rebuke the devourer for our sakes so that our crops are not destroyed and our fruit is not lost. (v. 11.) All nations will call us blessed, for we will be a delightful land. (v. 12.) That should be reason enough for any of us to trust the Lord and return to Him what is rightfully His.

Is your fruit being destroyed? Then why not be obedient to the Lord in your finances? Take Him at His Word. Put Him to the test with your tithes and offerings, and see if He will not do as He has promised.

You may think that you don't have enough for yourself and your family as it is without giving away what little you do have.

But God can multiply what you give back to Him. He can rebuke the devourer by seeing that the devil does not cause your old refrigerator to break down. He can keep that aged car from blowing up or falling apart. He can take that last half loaf of bread and that last half carton of milk for the baby and multiply it just as He did the loaves and fishes. (Matt. 14:14-21.) He can take your last tiny measure of rice and cause it to be replenished so that it never runs out, just as He did with the widow who was obedient enough to use her last bit of meal and oil to feed the prophet. (1 Kings 17:8-16.) There is no end to the miraculous ways in which the Lord can meet your most pressing needs — if you will trust Him to do so.

God can do more with your 10 percent than you could ever hope to do with the entire 100 percent. You are failing as it is now. Why not let Him see what He can do for you? Return to Him, and watch Him return to you!

Keep Yourself From the Curse

And ye, in any wise keep yourselves from the accursed thing, lest ye make yourselves accursed, when ye take of the accursed thing, and make the camp of Israel a curse, and trouble it.

But all the silver, and gold, and vessels of brass and iron, are consecrated unto the Lord: they shall come into the treasury of the Lord.

Joshua 6:18,19

In Deuteronomy 28:1-14, the Lord lists all the blessings that will come upon those who are careful to obey His commandments. Then in verses 15-68, He enumerates all the curses that will fall on those who are disobedient to Him. In the same way, in the third chapter of Malachi, the Lord promises blessings upon those who bring to Him the full tithe, warning in verse 9 that those who hold back the tithe bring a curse upon themselves.

In this passage from Joshua, we read again the Lord's warning about taking for our own use those holy things that belong to Him. When we knowingly withhold from the Lord what is His, we not only bring a curse upon ourselves, we trouble the whole camp — our family, our home, even our church.

Don't hold back from the Lord what is rightfully His. The price is too great to bear.

Tithe and Trust

> **Woe unto you, scribes and Pharisees, hypocrites! for ye pay tithe of mint and anise and cummin, and have omitted the weightier matters of the law, judgment, mercy, and faith: these ought ye to have done, and not to leave the other undone.**
>
> **Matthew 23:23**

In other words, the Lord is saying that although we are commanded to return the tithe to the Lord — as we should, and for which we will be blessed — that is not the end of our obligation or responsibility as Christians. We must go on to honor the Lord in other ways as well, such as showing justice and mercy to others and in being faithful in every aspect of our daily lives.

If we will heed the Word of the Lord, being careful to be obedient to Him in every way possible, including our tithes and offerings, He has promised that He will meet our needs and bless us abundantly.

The only way to become truly debt free is by *tithing* and *trusting!*

5
Things You Must Do to Be Successful

"For I know the plans that I have for you," declares the Lord, "plans for welfare and not for calamity to give you a future and a hope."
Jeremiah 29:11, NAS

God has a plan for you, a future for you. He has things planned for your good. God's plans for you are all good. He plans to bring you peace and prosperity, happiness and blessing. That is just the opposite of what some people think the future holds for them — especially many black people. Too often we African-Americans are told — or tell ourselves — that because we are born black, we will never have anything. I refuse to accept that. God's Word is not just for white people; it is for all of His children, whatever their color, race, or ethnic heritage.

God wants your mind to be set free. In the *New International Version* of this verse, the Lord says that He has **plans to prosper you and not to harm you, plans to give you hope and a future.** If it is God's plan to prosper you, then how can you say that your future is to have nothing just because you are black? That simply is not so! It is contrary to the written Word of God.

Those who believe that, those who think that God is after them, that He is out to get them, to keep them from having anything in life, that He is trying to teach them some lesson by depriving them of the good things of life — don't know what they are talking about. In His Word, God says that His people are destroyed for lack of knowledge. (Hos. 4:6.) If you are broke, if you have nothing, it is not because God is against you. It is because of a lack of God's Word in your mind and spirit.

To Give You Hope

Beloved, I wish above all things that thou mayest prosper and be in health, even as thy soul prospereth.

3 John 2

God plainly says that He wants us to prosper, that He has plans to give us hope and a future.

God wants you to have hope. That hope comes from knowing His Word. The reason many people are without is because they have a lack of knowledge concerning the will of God for them, His plan for them, what He wants them to have.

When your mind is renewed by the Word of God, it will cause you to prosper. When you begin to think the thoughts of God, you will begin to act like a God-kind of creature. That's why you can't lose when you get God's Word in you, because you will act like God.

When the devil tells you that God wants you to be on welfare for the rest of your life, you can stand up and tell him, "Devil, you're a liar. That is not God's plan for me. His plan is not for me to be on welfare, but for me to fare well!"

As a Man Thinketh

For as he thinketh in his heart, so is he. . . .

Proverbs 23:7

If you are on welfare right now, don't let that bother you. Just begin to get into the Word of God and let the Word of God get into you. As you do so, you will begin to renew your mind, to change your way of thinking. Your thoughts will begin to be transformed into the thoughts of God.

Don't run out and throw away your food stamps or refuse to accept your welfare checks. That's not what I am saying. Just begin to change your way of thinking about yourself and about God and His will and plan for you. Get it into your mind and heart that God *does* want you to prosper and be in health, just as your soul prospers. Begin to believe that God *does* want you to be a success, despite the situation in which you may find yourself at the moment.

Some people are on welfare because they have a welfare mentality. They think welfare, they talk welfare, they look welfare, they act welfare. Welfare is all they know. They have grown up on welfare. Their parents grew up on it. As far as they know, their family has always been on welfare — and always will be. They have such a welfare image and mindset that they cannot even conceive of themselves living any other way. The reason they live on welfare is because they have immersed themselves in welfare rather than in the Word and will and way of the Lord.

One time when I was laid off from work, I had to use food stamps for a while. Every time I went to cash my stamps, because I was so well dressed and well groomed, the lady treated me as though I was dishonest. I realized it was because I didn't look the part. So I actually began to change my appearance. I would wear faded, torn blue jeans and an old sweat-shirt when I went to buy groceries.

What had happened? I had begun to think welfare, talk welfare, live welfare. Welfare was in my heart. I was not just looking the part, I was living the part.

That's what the devil wants to do to you. He wants you to think welfare and look welfare and live welfare — forever.

But that is not God's will and plan for you. He wants you to think success, to look success, and to live success. He says so in His Word, and God cannot lie.

Be Renewed in Your Mind

> **And be not conformed to this world: but be ye transformed by the renewing of your mind, that ye may prove what is that good, and acceptable, and perfect, will of God.**
>
> **Romans 12:2**

Why do you think some people live in certain neighborhoods? Usually it is because those who think alike live alike. Just as water always seeks the lowest level, so people tend to seek their own level of thinking. They seek out those who have the same thought life.

During the first part of the time that I was laid off from General Motors, I was still drawing 95 percent of my salary while I looked for another job. I didn't want to find work. I was enjoying living it up and taking it easy. I loafed around until the money ran out, and then I didn't know what to do. A lady came up to me and said, "Brother Layton, this is not God's will for your life."

When I heard those words, something rose up in me and I got mad. I left that place in a huff. But later on, the Holy Spirit convicted me that the woman was telling the truth. That very day I started looking for a new job. I wanted to go to work someplace, anyplace. I also started studying the Scriptures and praying, "Lord," I asked, "What does she mean that this is not Your plan, Your will for me?"

What I learned was that it is God's will for me to prosper and succeed in life. That is His will for you, too. But in order for that will and plan to come to pass, there is something you must do. First of all, you must know that it is God's will for you to be prosperous and successful. Then you must believe it. You must renew your mind to His Word until your thinking is totally transformed so that your image of yourself comes into line with God's image of you.

The Wealth of the Sinner

...The wealth of the sinner is laid up for the just.
Proverbs 13:22

During the first few months that I was out of work, my family and I lived off of my father and mother. We did that so long that we got comfortable with it. As long as Momma and Daddy would hand out the groceries, we were happy to receive them. We didn't have any intention of doing anything else. We didn't try to find out God's plan for our lives. We didn't look for His "expected end" for us. We just "laid back and cruised."

You may be doing the same thing — "layin' back an' cruisin' " on your parents, or your friends, or the government. Like me, you may think that is all you will ever have or deserve — handouts, charity, welfare. If so, you have settled for the devil's lie. You have settled for less than God's best. You need to stand up and tell the devil that he is a liar. Tell him that you are going to discover God's plan for you, God's future for you, that you are going up and not down.

If you are out of work or in debt, you have no business going to the mall and buying things on credit. If you can't pay your bills, you don't need to be buying more things you cannot afford. Why should you buy a new car when you can't — or won't — pay for the one you have now? That's not faith. That's foolishness and stupidity.

If you have to ride a bicycle until God begins to prosper you, then ride a bike. Put some Armor All on it and make it shine. Make the very best of what you have, and wait on the Lord to provide you something better.

Maybe you have started tithing but you still have a couple of bills you haven't paid. Until you start meeting your obligations on time, God cannot release the fullness of His blessing on you even if you are returning to Him what you owe Him.

I can remember paying tithes and offerings but we still had unpaid bills stacked up. We were tithing regularly but it looked as if we would never prosper, because the bills kept piling in. I finally came to the point that I told my wife, "Honey, we have got to contact all these people we owe money to and tell them that we are going to start paying something on our account until we pay them off."

From that day, God started meeting our needs. He started sending in the money, making a way for us to pay what we owed.

Until you start being honest with everyone, you cannot be blessed. God cannot take the wealth of the wicked and give it to you if you are not right yourself. And if you are not paying your bills, you are not right;

you are a liar and a thief. God cannot and will not bless dishonesty.

As Thy Soul Prospereth

Remember, God said that He wishes above all things that we may prosper and be in health, even as our soul prospers.

The soul is often defined as the will, the emotions, and the mind or intellect. The reason you are not prospering is because your soul is not prospering. Your mind has not been renewed. Your emotions have not been brought under control. Your will is not right — not when you are ducking your creditors and not paying them what you owe. You can tithe and pledge and even give offerings until your tongue falls out, but if you are dishonest in your dealings with others, you will never prosper.

If you are not doing right and living right, not paying your tithe and giving offerings, not paying your debts and being honest in all your dealings, you open a door to the devil to rob you of your blessings. Remember, God's law is that what you sow is what you will reap. You may be blessed to a degree, but the real blessings, that thing that will put you over, that thing that will cause you to enter the promised land, that thing that will cause you to eat the good of the land and to know the good, acceptable and perfect will of the Lord — that thing will be held up.

I had to learn that lesson the hard way. When I did, I told my wife that we would never have anything unless we paid the Lord what we owed Him and then paid everyone else what we owed them. We vowed that from that day forward we were going to do right and live right. I didn't want people saying, "There goes Rick Layton. He preaches prosperity and success, yet he won't even pay his bills. He goes around telling people that they've got to be saved and live right, and he himself is a thief and a robber."

It took us years to pay off the bills we owed. But with God's help, we did. The Lord blessed us and now we are free. You, too, can get debt free, if you will renew your mind to the Word and will of God, and then live that Word in your day-to-day dealings.

God Takes Pleasure in Your Prosperity

> **Let them shout for joy, and be glad, that favour my righteous cause: yea, let them say continually, Let the Lord be magnified, which hath pleasure in the prosperity of his servant.**
>
> **Psalm 35:27**

It is God's will for all of His children to prosper and be successful. He takes pleasure in their prosperity — just as we take pleasure in the well-being and happiness of our children.

But in order for God to prosper us, we must live right. We live right by being honest with God and with our fellow man. We live right by giving the Lord what we owe Him and paying others what we owe them. It is just that simple. Until you are willing to do that — and begin to make an effort to do that — you can forget about being truly blessed and prospered because that is God's way. I know, because I learned it on my own. Once I started living right and doing things God's way, I began to prosper. And the same will be true for you.

Cast Thy Bread

> **Cast thy bread upon the waters: for thou shalt find it after many days.**
>
> **Ecclesiastes 11:1**

This verse simply means that we must be willing to let go if we are to receive. One way we let go is by giving to others what is rightfully theirs. God cannot fill a clenched fist. If we are to receive the fullness that God wants to pour into our lives, we must open our hands and our hearts. We must truly let go and let God.

This is the lesson my wife and I learned. We discovered that we had to let go and make a start at least on paying back what we owed our creditors. As we did so, God began to move on our behalf. He began to bless us so that eventually we were able to pay off everything we owed. We became debt free because we did as the Lord commanded. We learned that if we expect God to do His part, then we must be willing and obedient to do our part. Until then, nothing happens.

It took us ten years to get to the place that we could shout with joy because the Lord had truly taken pleasure in the prosperity of His servants. You can know that same feeling and have that same experience, but only if you are willing to do what we did and be obedient to the Lord. You can't prosper if you are not willing to favor the Lord's righteous cause.

Making vows is wonderful. It gives you a point of contact. But you can make vows all you want. If you are not willing to keep your vows, then you will never receive God's best. God wants you to magnify Him in the earth. You do that by being obedient to do His will.

God has a plan for you, but you've got to work God's plan.

Seek the Lord and His Will

The young lions do lack, and suffer hunger: but

they that seek the Lord shall not want any good thing.
Psalm 34:10

Sometimes the lion goes without his meal. But you and I can say with the psalmist, **The Lord is my shepherd; I shall not want.** (Ps. 23:1.) *The Living Bible* says, **Because the Lord is my Shepherd, I have everything I need!**

A shepherd oversees the flock under his care, making sure the sheep are walking in the right path. God is our Great Shepherd. He wants to direct our course, making sure that we walk in the right way. Because He is our Shepherd, our Guide, our Director and our Provider, He has assured us that we will not lack any good thing.

But as with all God's assurances, there is a condition to that promise. No shepherd can protect and keep and provide for a sheep that will not be obedient to hear and heed his voice. In the same way, you and I are assured of the provision and protection of our Divine Shepherd only to the extent that we are willing to listen and follow. When we go astray, when we are disobedient, when we stubbornly follow our own way, then we take ourselves out of the protection of the sheepfold and open ourselves to attack from the devourer.

If we want to prosper and be in health, even as our soul prospers, then we must keep ourselves from the evil one. If the devil has anything he can use against us, he will. God's blessings are for all His children — all His *obedient* children. God's will is for us to be prosperous and successful. We will be — if we are careful to do the things that lead to prosperity and success God's way.

6

The Definition of Success

Sixteen years old was Uzziah when he began to reign, and he reigned fifty and two years in Jerusalem. . . .

And he did that which was right in the sight of the Lord, according to all that his father Amaziah did.
2 Chronicles 26:3,4

One of the definitions of the adjective *successful* is "the obtaining of that which one desires or intends." The noun form, *success,* is defined as "a favorable or desired outcome of something attempted." Finally, the verb form, *to succeed,* is defined as "to prosper, to accomplish one's goals, to reach one's objectives."

Don't you want to be successful in life, to obtain that which you desire or intend? Don't you want a favorable outcome to your endeavors? Don't you want to succeed — to prosper, to accomplish your goals, to reach your objectives?

Of course, you do. Everyone does. No one wants to be a failure, nor do we want our children to fail.

The same is true of our heavenly Father. He wants us to succeed even more than we want our children to be successful.

But in order for us to be successful in life, we have seen that there are certain things we must do, certain things that God desires and requires of us. The first one we discussed is that God demands that we pay our debts — to Him and to others.

God wants His children to be honest, to keep their word, to pay their bills. God cannot and will not bless and prosper an individual who is dishonest or disobedient. If we want the Lord to cause us to succeed, then we must do as King Uzziah. We must do that which is right in the sight of the Lord.

Miracle Money and Debt Cancellation

And he sought God in the days of Zechariah, who had understanding in the visions of God: and as long as he sought the Lord, God made him to prosper.
2 Chronicles 26:5

It is senseless of Christians to run around talking about miracle money or debt cancellation without living right and doing right. The only way God can perform a financial miracle or cancel a person's debt is for that individual to do what's right in His sight. As we have said again and again, God does not reward dishonesty nor does He bless disobedience.

As long as King Uzziah sought the Lord, God blessed him and made him to prosper.

What would cause anyone to think that he could not seek the Lord, not put God first, and that the Lord would still cause him to prosper? We could turn this statement around and make it into a prosperity and success principle: If any person does *not* seek God, does *not* put God first, then God will *not* make him to prosper.

Just as the law of sowing and reaping states that whatever a person sows, that shall he also reap, this law declares that as long as an individual seeks the Lord, He will cause that person to prosper.

That is God's law, His plan, for you and me just as much as it was for King Uzziah. If we want to prosper, we must seek the Lord. We must go after Him with our whole heart. We must put Him first in our lives, in everything we say and do.

Prosperity Requires Honesty

> **He that covereth his sins shall not prosper: but whoso confesseth and forsaketh them shall have mercy.**
>
> **Proverbs 28:13**

I am so sick of people ministering prosperity and success without saying anything about living right. There is much more to success and prosperity than simply following the ABCs of tithing and making vows. It is true that there is no way to prosper without tithing and giving offerings, but there is no way to prosper without living right either — and that includes paying what you owe.

If you are in debt to someone, if you have bills that you have not paid, then you are under obligation. You have given your word to that person that you will repay him for what you have received from him. There is no way to duck that responsibility and still receive God's blessing. God cannot and will not make a robber and a thief prosperous. That would make God as big a cheat and a crook as the one who refuses to pay his debts.

You must live right for God to prosper you. If you see a dishonest person prospering, he is prospering his own way. Those of us who are children of God must live right if we are to be prosperous and successful. That is an unchangeable spiritual law.

The Lord has decreed in His Word that whoever covers or hides his sins will not prosper. He could have said that whoever ducks the bill collector will not prosper. The principle is the same. But He also says that whoever confesses and forsakes sin will have mercy. That means that if you are in debt and start paying off what you owe, then you can begin to prosper again.

Start doing what is right, and you will begin to prosper. God will give you miracle money and cancel your debt — but He will do it His way, as you are obedient to His will and His Word.

God has an order: You must work with Him. Unless you are willing to keep your word to others, don't expect God to keep His Word to you. It is just that simple. When you buy something on credit, you have received something of value for which you have promised to repay. If you don't do that, then you have broken your word. You are a liar. You are also holding on to or have used up something that does not belong to you. So you are also a thief. And no one trusts a liar and a thief.

When you go to apply for credit, you are asked to fill out certain forms so your past record can be checked. You are being tested to see if you are a person of integrity, to see if your word is any good. If you have a bad record, then you need to start doing something to change it. You need to get yourself straightened out because there is fast coming a time when cash won't do much good. In the future, we are going to be living by credit cards. And those who can't qualify because of their past history are going to be in serious trouble.

In today's society, you can't even rent a car without a major credit card. Ours is quickly becoming a plastic society. Soon we won't be able to fly on an airplane or buy clothing or pay for a meal in a restaurant without our name being in a computer system. Anyone without a good credit rating is in for hard times ahead.

You Reap What You Sow

If a son shall ask bread of any of you that is a father, will he give him a stone? or if he ask a fish, will he for a fish give him a serpent?

Or if he shall ask an egg, will he offer him a scorpion?

Luke 11:11,12

I used to preach that when you give tithes and offerings, sometimes God blesses you in a spiritual way. But the Bible says that whatever a person sows is exactly what he will reap. (Gal. 6:7.) That means that if you sow money, then you will reap money. What you put in determines what will come back out. That's important to know when you are sowing for a certain crop.

If that were not true, then we couldn't trust our money to God because we could never know what we were going to get in return for our giving. If we needed new furniture and we gave money, we might get back some kind of spiritual blessing that would not meet our material need at all.

Jesus taught that whatever we ask of the Father, that is exactly what He will give us. David, the psalmist, said that if we delight ourselves in the Lord, He will give us the desires of our heart. (Ps. 37:4.) My desire is just like that of King Uzziah. I seek the Lord, and because I do, He causes me to prosper.

I can't go to church and dance in the Spirit and get my bills paid. My creditors don't want sweat. They want money. I can't offer them tongues or prophecies or visions. I have to have hard cash. So when I sow my money into the work of the Lord, then I expect money in return.

> **God is not a man, that he should lie; neither the son of man, that he should repent. . . .**
>
> **Numbers 23:19**

He has promised that when we give, *what we have given will be returned to us,* good measure, pressed down, shaken together, and running over. (Luke 6:38.) He is talking about money. That means there is nothing wrong with money. Scripture says **the love of money is a root of all kinds of evil. . . .** (1 Tim. 6:10, NIV.) But it's not necessary to have money to love it. Some of the biggest money worshippers are those who have absolutely nothing.

As someone has said, the only thing worse than the love of money is the lack of money. I agree. It is hard to shout and praise and worship God when you're broke. When money becomes a burden, then it is no longer a blessing. It takes money to pay bills. It takes money to live. The Lord knows that. That's why He has commanded us to sow and reap, to give to meet the needs of others, *expecting to receive in return* so that our own needs may be met. That is the basic purpose of the law of sowing and reaping.

Charge Them That Are Rich

> **Charge them that are rich in this world, that they be not highminded, nor trust in uncertain riches, but in the living God, who giveth us richly all things to enjoy;**
>
> **That they do good, that they be rich in good works, ready to distribute, willing to communicate.**
>
> **1 Timothy 6:17,18**

Paul teaches that we are not to trust in money but in God. We are to be rich in good works, ready to distribute to others, willing to communicate or share with those around us.

But how can we give what we don't have? We may be willing, but if we have nothing to give, will our willingness be of any use or value to anyone else — or to ourselves? That's why it is God's will and plan that we be prosperous — so we will have enough to be generous on every occasion. That's why He instituted the principle of sowing and reaping, so we can use our physical possessions to produce more for others and to meet our own needs.

God Will Make a Way

Thus saith the Lord, which maketh a way in the sea, and a path in the mighty waters.

Isaiah 43:16

If you will be obedient to the Lord, He will pass over the disobedient to get to you, to make a way for you. He will open up doors for you that no man can close. (Is. 22:22.) But you must trust Him, put Him first, do what is right in His sight.

We must quit living half-heartedly and thinking that we are going to be abundantly blessed of the Lord just because we are His children or because we tithe or even give offerings. It just doesn't work that way. God is for all His people. He hasn't just picked you and me out to bless. He wants to prosper all those who call upon His name. But He can only bless and prosper those who will do what He has commanded them to do. And the first thing He has commanded us to do is to be honest — with Him and with others.

Look Forward, Not Back

Remember ye not the former things, neither consider the things of old.

Behold, I will do a new thing; now it shall spring forth; shall ye not know it? I will even make a way in the wilderness, and rivers in the desert.

This people have I formed for myself; they shall shew forth my praise.

Isaiah 43:18,19,21

"Forget about the past," says the Lord. "Forget about the heartaches and the fears. Forget about the times you couldn't pay your bills. Forget all that. Now that you have learned to put your trust in Me, look to the future, for I have great plans for you. I will do a new thing in your life. I will make a way for you in the wilderness of your current situation. I will bring you out so that you can show forth My praise in the world."

This is our time. God is going to begin to open to us a way of life that will cause us to shine forth as a beacon of light to all those who stumble in darkness. God says that when an individual's ways are pleasing to Him, He makes even that person's enemies to live in peace with him. (Prov. 16:7.) But it is also true that if a person does not live in a way that is pleasing to God, then his enemies will come in and take everything he has.

Be Not Weary in Well-Doing

And let us not be weary in well-doing: for in due season we shall reap, if we faint not.

Galatians 6:9

We must never become weary in well-doing, never get tired of doing what is right. God has promised to establish our goings, to set our feet on a rock, to cause us to eat the best of the land.

Too many times people hear all these promises and jump and shout in church, but then go out and live in the world just as if none of this is true or has any meaning. They forget to put God first so He can put them first.

I am not preaching anything that I don't practice. I have heard it said by some businessmen and bankers that preachers are the worst credit risks of all their clients. Others seem to have the same opinion of Christians in general. That is not pleasing to God. Our heavenly Father does not want His children to have such a miserable reputation. He wants us to be honest and to pay our debts. He wants us to be people of honor and integrity — just as He is a God of honor and integrity.

If you want to prosper, if you want to succeed, if you want to obtain that which you desire or intend, then do what God says to do. Put Him first. Render unto God what is God's and unto others what is due them. If you will do that, the Lord will fulfill His gracious Word to you and give you the ability to get wealth in order to establish His covenant in the earth.

That is success as God defines it.

7

God Can Be Trusted to Honor His Word

Owe no man any thing, but to love one another: for he that loveth another hath fulfilled the law.
Romans 13:8

Too many times people are so concerned with God canceling their debt that they fail to give Him anything to work with.

When the Lord looks down from heaven, does He see that you are doing your part to cancel your own debt? You can't expect God to do for you what it is your duty and responsibility to do for yourself. You got yourself into debt, and you must make the effort to get yourself out.

It is true that King Uzziah and others were prospered by the Lord, but it was because they were seeking Him, not what He could give them or do for them. God is not a celestial Santa Claus or a genie of the lamp who is obligated to rush forth to do our bidding and cover all our debts.

Those whom God prospers fulfill their part of the bargain by doing what is right in His sight. And it is right in God's sight to make an honest effort to start repaying what is owed — to Him and to others.

Don't try to duck the collection plate or your bill collectors. That is not right in the sight of God. Pay your tithe first, and then pay what you can on your other debts. Be realistic. Look to the Lord to help you get totally out of debt step by step — not by pouring "miracle money" out upon you from heaven.

And be careful to live right in every other way. You are not seeking God if you are engaged in sin. Jesus warned that everything we do in secret will be brought to the light. But He also promised that whatever good we do in secret will be openly rewarded by the Father.

We have been promised prosperity, but as with King Uzziah, how much we prosper depends on what we seek.

Seek Those Things Which Are Above

> **If ye then be risen with Christ, seek those things which are above, where Christ sitteth on the right hand of God.**
>
> **Set your affection on things above, not on things on the earth.**
>
> **Colossians 3:1,2**

In these verses, the Lord is telling us the same thing He told Uzziah — that we are to seek Him rather than His blessings. We are to set our affection on things above, not on things of the earth.

In Matthew 6:31-33, Jesus commanded that we seek first God and His righteousness, assuring us that when we do, all the things we need will be added unto us. If we want to prosper, we must be careful what we seek. Prosperity and success are by-products of seeking the Lord. They come as a result of placing our affection on things above, not on things below.

As long as King Uzziah sought the Lord, he was prospered. As long as he put God first in everything he did, God caused him to prosper and succeed. The same will be true of us. If we want to be prosperous and successful in life, then we must seek, not prosperity and success, but the Lord Himself. It is not the provisions we are to seek after, but the Provider.

In 2 Timothy 2:15, we are told: **Study to shew thyself approved unto God, a workman that needeth not to be ashamed, rightly dividing the word of truth.** If there is a right way to divide the word of truth, then there must be a wrong way. Some of us have got hold of certain scriptures about prosperity and success in which there is an element of truth. But too often we have misinterpreted and misapplied these passages because we have taken them out of context and made them say something that God never intended.

God wants us to prosper and succeed in life, just as Uzziah did. He has plainly said so in His Word. But He wants us to have the right priorities. He wants us to put first things first. He wants us to seek Him and His righteousness rather than the things of this earth. He has promised that if we will seek those things that are above, then He will provide those things that He knows we need.

And God can be trusted to keep His Word!

God Can Be Trusted

The Lord said to me, "You have seen correctly, for I am watching to see that my word is fulfilled."
Jeremiah 1:12, NIV

In the *King James Version,* the Lord says, **...I will hasten my word to perform it.**

When you become a doer of the Word, God will move on your behalf. God said He watches over His

Word to see that it is fulfilled. He hastens to perform it. When you put God first, as He has commanded, then He puts you first, as He has promised.

The Bible says that we serve a God Who does not lie. (Num. 23:19.) If you do the Word of God and He fails to do what He has promised, then He is a liar. But that will not happen because Hebrews 6:18 tells us that it is impossible for God to lie.

So if you do the Word, God is honor-bound to bless you. His integrity will not allow Him to break His promise. There is no such thing as a tither who does not get repaid. There is no such thing as a person who gives offerings without receiving more than what he has given.

There is also no such thing as a person who cannot put his trust and hope in God. When an individual refuses to do the Word of God, he is saying to the Lord, "I don't trust You. You don't watch over Your Word to perform it."

If you don't trust God, you can't expect to receive from Him.

Where Is Your Treasure?

> **Lay not up for yourselves treasures upon earth, where moth and rust doth corrupt, and where thieves break through and steal:**
>
> **But lay up for yourselves treasures in heaven, where neither moth nor rust doth corrupt, and where thieves do not break through nor steal:**
>
> **For where your treasure is, there will your heart be also.**
>
> **Matthew 6:19-21**

Jesus said that where our treasure is, there our hearts will be also. The Apostle Paul says that we should keep our eyes on those things that are above, not on the things that are in the earth.

Where is your treasure? Where is your affection? Is it on things above or below? Have you stored up heavenly treasures? Have you put God first in everything you do?

Where is your heart? Is it in God or in things? If your heart is in God, then no one has to make you do anything. No one has to bribe you to do what is right. You want to do the will of the Lord because you want to please your heavenly Father. You want to be obedient to the Word of God, whether it brings you a reward or not. If the Word says to do something, you do it because you want to — not because you have to or as a means of getting something out of God.

Attitude is such an important part of serving the Lord. Without the right attitude of heart, no one can ever hope or expect to be truly blessed by the Lord — no matter how much he gives or how many good deeds he performs in his life.

It is not God's blessings we are to seek, but God Himself. Blessings flow naturally to those whose primary purpose in life is to seek after God and His righteousness. That is what Jesus is saying to us in Matthew 6.

Nevertheless, At Thy Word....

So then faith cometh by hearing, and hearing by the word of God.

Romans 10:17

When Jesus commanded Peter and his friends to cast their nets on the other side of the boat, they answered, **Master, we have toiled all the night, and have taken nothing: nevertheless at thy word...** (Luke 5:5).

They were saying, "Master, we don't have any evidence to go on. We don't even understand what You're talking about. We are professional fishermen. We have spent our lives fishing these waters. We just came in here from fishing all night. We know there are no fish here.

"What do You know about fishing anyway? You're a carpenter. Nevertheless, because we have seen You multiply the loaves and fishes that were placed into Your hands, because we have seen You work miracles and heal those who were sick and perform great wonders, we trust Your Word. We will do as You say and leave the consequences to You."

The outcome was far beyond anything the disciples could have ever imagined. The same will be true for us when we act in faith.

But where do we get this faith? The Bible says that faith comes by hearing, and hearing by the Word of God. When we get the Word of God into us, it will come alive in our spirit. It will instruct and equip and energize us so that we will have everything we need to accomplish whatever God commands us to do. We will know that it is God's will and plan for us to be prosperous and successful.

We will also know that if we are to have the things we need to do God's work on this earth, we must do things His way. Our treasure will be in heaven, not on earth. Our eyes will be on things above, not on things below. Our priorities will be in order. We will seek God and His Kingdom and His righteousness first. We will want to do right, because we will want to be pleasing to God.

All of these things will come to pass as a result of trusting the Word of God. As we learn to receive and do the Word, we will be blessed. We will do what we love, and it will produce good results. We will be prosperous and successful. We will be healthy, wealthy and wise. We will be given the very desires of our heart, because our heart will be in the right place.

Remember to put God first in all you do. Make Him your delight, and He will give you the desires of your heart. Seek Him, and you will have treasures in heaven and blessings now while you are in the earth. You will be enriched in every way so that you can be generous to every good work.

All you have to do is take God at His Word — and then do His Word.

The Lord Will Be With You

And the Lord was with Joseph, and he was a prosperous man; and he was in the house of his master the Egyptian.

Genesis 39:2

Any time the Lord is with a person, you can be assured that individual is doing something right. Yet we see that, although God was with Joseph so that he was a prosperous man, he was in bondage to Potiphar, the Egyptian.

God will bless and prosper you if you live right in another man's house or in someone else's system. The system under which you and I live is not God's. It was set up by man. But even in this situation, God will make us prosperous if we will do as Joseph and be willing and obedient to God's commands.

He Will Make You Prosperous

And his master saw that the Lord was with him,

and that the Lord made all that he did to prosper in his hand.

Genesis 39:3

God can bless you and prosper you even while you are on welfare or even while you serve a hard taskmaster. He can move upon those who are in positions of authority and power over you and cause you to have favor with them, just as He did for Joseph. But in order for that to happen, you must do as Joseph did and be a responsible, hard-working, honest, reliable servant. Wherever Joseph found himself, he worked hard and made a name for himself as a faithful and trustworthy servant, and God blessed him for it.

If you will be faithful and patient like Joseph, one day you will be led out of bondage just as he was. But it will be through a process over a period of time. Even the Old Testament saints like Joseph and David had to prove themselves before they were promoted and exalted. That's why I caution you not to expect things to fall from heaven upon you, but to be diligent to do your part as you work with the Lord in coming forth out of bondage into freedom and abundance. As you do so, God will cause others to see that He is with you and that it is He Who is causing you to prosper. That will bring glory to God and honor to you, just as it did in Joseph's case. That, too, is part of God's plan.

Joseph Found Grace, Brought Blessing and Won Favor

And Joseph found grace in his sight, and he served him: and he made him overseer over his house, and all that he had he put into his hand.

And it came to pass from the time that he had made him overseer in his house, and over all that he had, that the Lord blessed the Egyptian's house for

Joseph's sake; and the blessing of the Lord was upon all that he had in the house, and in the field.

And he left all that he had in Joseph's hand; and he knew not aught he had, save the bread which he did eat. And Joseph was a goodly person, and well favoured.

Genesis 39:4-6

Because Joseph was such a faithful servant, he found grace in the eyes of his master who soon put him in charge of everything in his household.

The Bible says in verse 5, **it came to pass.** It will come to pass in your life, too, if you do as Joseph did and live right in whatever circumstances you may find yourself.

The Lord blessed the Egyptian for Joseph's sake. God is blessing your home, your family, your neighborhood, your church, your city, your company, your nation for your sake. That's how much God loves you. He has every hair of your head numbered. Every good thing you have has come directly from His loving hands. All of the earth's resources — the silver and the gold and the cattle on a thousand hills — belong to God. He gives it to whomever He wills. The only reason those in authority over you are being blessed and prospered is because of you. God is taking pleasure in the prosperity of His servant. He is pouring out His blessing on you and your employers just as He did with Joseph. All this is happening because you are a righteous person and are well favored.

When you are pleasing to the Lord, everyone around you is blessed. Like faithful Abraham, you are not only blessed, you are a blessing to many others. In fact, that's why God blesses you, so you can be a blessing. That, too, is part of God's plan.

The Reason For Prosperity

> **But thou shalt remember the Lord thy God: for it is he that giveth thee power to get wealth, that he may establish his covenant which he sware unto thy fathers, as it is this day.**
>
> **Deuteronomy 8:18**

We do not prosper because of our own efforts, but because the Lord gives us the power to get wealth so that He may establish His covenant in the earth.

In the Old Testament, we see that the majority of God's great men were wealthy. For example, we read in Genesis 13:2 that Abram **...was very rich in cattle, in silver, and in gold.** Why did God bless Abram so much? So he could be a blessing to many others. (Gen. 12:3.)

God Promised Blessings

> **And it shall come to pass, if thou shalt hearken diligently unto the voice of the Lord thy God, to observe and to do all his commandments...that the Lord thy God will set thee on high above all nations of the earth:**
>
> **And all these blessings shall come on thee, and overtake thee, if thou shalt hearken unto the voice of the Lord thy God.**
>
> **Blessed shalt thou be in the city, and blessed shalt thou be in the field.**
>
> **Blessed shall be the fruit of thy body, and the fruit of thy ground, and the fruit of thy cattle, the increase of thy kine, and the flocks of thy sheep.**
>
> **Blessed shall be thy basket and thy store.**
>
> **Blessed shalt thou be when thou comest in, and blessed shalt thou be when thou goest out.**
>
> **Deuteronomy 28:1-6**

It is God's plan for you and me to be rich both in spiritual blessings and in material blessings and to be healthy in our physical bodies.

Does that mean that you are going to be a millionaire? I don't know. But I do know that God wants you to have enough to be able to pay your bills, return your tithes, give offerings and give to the work of the Gospel. That's all you really need. You don't have to have a huge bank account to be prosperous. All that's necessary is enough to meet your own needs and the needs of those whom God entrusts to you.

In Matthew 6:9-13, the Lord Jesus said that we are to pray for our daily bread — not our daily cake. In the last part of that prayer, He indicated that we should pray for God's will to be done on earth as it is in heaven. God's will is that His covenant be established on earth so that people can get a glimpse of heaven.

Is there any sickness in heaven?

Is there any poverty in heaven? No. Is there life and health and abundance in heaven? Yes. Then that is God's will. That is what God wants for us here and now.

Blessings and Cursings

> **The Lord shall command the blessing upon thee in thy storehouses, and in all that thou settest thine hand unto; and he shall bless thee in the land which the Lord thy God giveth thee.**
>
> **And the Lord shall make thee plenteous in goods, in the fruit of thy body, and in the fruit of thy cattle, and in the fruit of thy ground....**
>
> **The Lord shall open unto thee his good treasure, the heaven to give the rain unto thy land in his season, and to bless all the work of thine hand: and thou shalt lend unto many nations, and thou shalt not borrow.**
>
> **And the Lord shall make thee the head, and not the tail; and thou shalt be above only, and thou shalt not be beneath; if that thou hearken unto the commandments of the Lord thy God....**
>
> **Deuteronomy 28:8,11-13**

God wants us to have nice things. That's part of the redemption package. Salvation is more than just heaven. It is prosperity, health and abundant life here and now.

Right after all the blessings of obedience are listed in Deuteronomy 28, the Lord describes all the curses that will come upon those who do not obey Him and do not walk in His ways. When people are *disobedient* to God, they *bring* the *curse* of the law *upon themselves.* But those of us who are in Christ have been redeemed from the curse. (Gal. 3:13.) We have been redeemed from poverty and lack. We have become heirs of God and joint-heirs of Christ. (Rom. 8:17.) Everything that belongs to God has now become ours. (1 Cor. 3:21-23.) And He has promised to bless us with it, if we are faithful and obedient.

God wants us to be blessed so that we can be a blessing. He wants us to have everything we need to go into all the world and preach the Gospel to every creature. And all of that will be ours, if we will simply trust the Lord to honor His Word.

8
How to Enter the Realm of Success

> **Wherefore, if God so clothe the grass of the field, which to-day is, and to-morrow is cast into the oven, shall he not much more clothe you, O ye of little faith?**
>
> **Therefore take no thought, saying, What shall we eat, or, What shall we drink? or, Wherewithal shall we be clothed?**
>
> **(For after all these things do the Gentiles seek:) for your heavenly Father knoweth that ye have need of all these things.**
>
> **Matthew 6:30-32**

One of the ways to enter into the realm of success is by obeying Matthew 6:30-33. God knows that we have need of food and drink and clothes. He is fully aware that we need a home and protection and security. He is not oblivious to the fact that we are human beings and must be continually provided with sustenance and shelter if we are to survive.

Why do we think that God would ever leave us or forsake us? What makes us think that God either does not know or does not care that we must be continually provided for? Especially when He has plainly told us that if we will seek Him first, then He will add unto us all these necessities of life.

God knows that we have needs, and He has promised to meet those needs. What other assurance can He give?

I have children. Don't you think that as a loving parent I am going to do all in my power to provide for them the things they need to live day by day? Am I better than God? Am I more loving or more concerned or more conscientious or more trustworthy than He? Am I more willing or able to provide for my children than our heavenly Father is to provide for His children?

God is fully able to care for those who place themselves in His hands. He is the richest person I know. The Bible tells us that everything belongs to Him — the silver and the gold and the cattle on a thousand hills. Everything that exists — including us — belongs to God. Is He then unable to provide for His own offspring? Is He any less willing to do so than we are to provide for our children?

Qualifying For God's Provision

> **But seek ye first the kingdom of God, and his righteousness; and all these things shall be added unto you.**
>
> **Matthew 6:33**

This is the qualification for receiving from God all the things that we need: *Seek first His Kingdom and His righteousness.*

One reason we have so many problems and so much hardship is because we are not doing what the Lord has prescribed. In fact, we are doing just the opposite. We are seeking after "all these things" instead of seeking after God's Kingdom and His righteousness.

God is not opposed to His children being blessed and prospered. He is not against us having things. He just doesn't want things to have us. That's why He did not say that money was the root of all evil, but that *the love of money* is the root of all kinds of evil.

God knows that we need money, food, drink, clothing, shelter, transportation and many other good things of life. He has even promised to provide them for us. But He has also told us how we are to go about qualifying ourselves to receive these good things He wants to give us. That is by putting Him first in our lives.

All we have to do is put God first, to seek Him before anything else, to get and remain in right standing with Him. The way we do that is by accepting Jesus Christ as Savior and Lord and then walking in His righteousness.

Righteousness: Key to Prosperity

Blessed are they which do hunger and thirst after righteousness: for they shall be filled.

Matthew 5:6

Do you realize that Jesus is saying the same thing in Matthew 6:33 that He said in Matthew 5:6 — that those who seek after God and His righteousness will be filled? That those who hunger and thirst after God and His Kingdom will receive everything they need in this life?

If you are not being blessed abundantly, if you are not being filled day by day, then you must not be hungering and thirsting after righteousness, you must not be seeking first God and His Kingdom.

Jesus did not say that if we seek God's Kingdom and His righteousness then all these things we need *might* be added unto us. He said they *shall* be added unto us. Neither did He say that if we hunger and thirst after righteousness, we *might* be filled. He said that we *shall* be filled.

If you and I will begin to hunger and thirst after righteousness, if we will begin to seek the Lord with our whole heart, if we will put first God and His Kingdom, then I can assure you that He *will* begin to add unto us all the things we need and that we *will* be filled. I can guarantee it, because He has guaranteed it.

When we buy an expensive item, like tires for our car, we look for a warranty, a guarantee. If one is not provided, then we probably won't purchase that product. You and I have come to rely on warranties and guarantees to assure us that we are getting what we pay for. Why then are we so cautious about accepting the guarantees that the Lord offers us? Why do we trust the word of other people who are out to sell us something more than we trust the Word of our heavenly Father Who is out to give us something? It doesn't make sense.

Praise the Lord Who Rescues Us

> **I waited patiently for the Lord; and he inclined unto me, and heard my cry.**
>
> **He brought me up also out of an horrible pit, out of the miry clay, and set my feet upon a rock, and established my goings.**
>
> **And he hath put a new song in my mouth, even praise unto our God: many shall see it, and fear, and shall trust in the Lord.**
>
> **Psalm 40:1-3**

God is waiting to bring us up out of a horrible pit, out of the miry clay, to set our feet on a rock, to establish our goings, to put a new song in our mouth, even praise unto Him — just as He did for David.

And that new song will be the doxology:

Praise God, from whom ALL blessings flow;
Praise Him ALL creatures here below;
Praise Him above, ye heavenly host;
Praise Father, Son, and Holy Ghost.

Who Can Be Against Us?

What shall we then say to these things? If God be for us, who can be against us?

Romans 8:31

God is not against us, He is for us. It is His desire that we prosper and be in health, just as our soul prospers. It is His plan to do good to us, not evil, to give us hope and a future. God is on our side.

It is Satan who is our enemy, not God. It is the devil who hates us and opposes us and troubles us and causes us difficulty. Jesus said that the enemy comes to steal, and to kill, and to destroy, but that He, the Son of God, came that we might have life in all its fullness and abundance. (John 10:10.)

Then He went on to tell us how to receive and live in and enjoy that fullness, that abundant life: *Seek first the Kingdom of God and His righteousness.*

That is the only requirement — to seek God first. And the way to seek God first is to get into His Word and walk in obedience to it.

Seeking God Brings Wealth

And Abram went up out of Egypt, he, and his wife, and all that he had, and Lot with him, into the south.

And Abram was very rich in cattle, in silver, and in gold.

And he went on his journeys from the south even to Bethel, unto the place where his tent had been at the beginning, between Bethel and Hai;

Unto the place of the altar, which he had made there at the first: and there Abram called on the name of the Lord.

And Lot also, which went with Abram, had flocks, and herds, and tents.

> **And the land was not able to bear them, that they might dwell together: for their substance was great, so that they could not dwell together.**
>
> **Genesis 13:1-6**

In this passage, we see that because Abram called upon the Lord, he and his entire family — including his nephew, Lot — were enormously blessed and prospered by the Lord.

It is God's will for you and me to enjoy the same blessings that He poured out upon Abraham and Lot and Jacob and all of the other Old Testament saints who put God and His Kingdom first.

The Disciples as Prosperous Men

> **Now as he walked by the sea of Galilee, he saw Simon and Andrew his brother casting a net into the sea: for they were fishers.**
>
> **And Jesus said unto them, Come ye after me, and I will make you to become fishers of men.**
>
> **And straightway they forsook their nets, and followed him.**
>
> **And when he had gone a little further thence, he saw James the son of Zebedee, and John his brother, who also were in the ship mending their nets.**
>
> **And straightway he called them: and they left their father Zebedee in the ship with the hired servants, and went after him.**
>
> **Mark 1:16-20**

As we can see in this passage, the men who followed Jesus were not poor. If they had paid servants working for them, then they must have been fairly prosperous businessmen. You can't hire others to work for you if you have nothing.

Later, in Luke 18:28, Peter said to the Lord, **...Lo, we have left all, and followed thee.** You must have something in order to leave something. In response to Peter's statement, Jesus assured him that anyone who left anything for His sake would be rewarded many times over (vv. 29,30.)

The fact that these men left their father to carry on the work of fishing while they went off to follow Jesus is also a good indication that they were financially stable. No one can afford to go and minister for three years without having some kind of continuing income. These men had to take care of their families.

We know from Scripture, for example, that Peter had a wife and a mother-in-law to care for. (Matt. 8:14,15; Mark 1:30,31.) Surely more of these men had to send something home to provide for their families' needs. The Bible says that a person who won't take care of his own household is worse than an infidel. (1 Tim. 5:8.) Jesus provided for them while they were following Him in ministry, but they had to have money to take care of those they had left behind.

In the same way, the Lord will provide for those of us who follow after and serve Him today. No one ever starved to death serving God. But as Jesus did with the disciples, He does call upon us to put Him first. Sometimes that means leaving behind or giving up certain things that we hold dear in order to fulfill His call on our lives, as we see in the case of the apostles who were obedient — and the rich young ruler who wasn't.

Put God First

And when he was gone forth into the way, there came one running, and kneeled to him, and asked

him, Good Master, what shall I do that I may inherit eternal life?

And Jesus said unto him, Why callest thou me good? there is none good but one, that is, God.

Thou knowest the commandments, Do not commit adultery, Do not kill, Do not steal, Do not bear false witness, Defraud not, Honour thy father and mother.

And he answered and said unto him, Master, all these have I observed from my youth.

Then Jesus beholding him loved him, and said unto him, One thing thou lackest: go thy way, sell whatsoever thou hast, and give to the poor, and thou shalt have treasure in heaven: and come, take up thy cross, and follow me.

And he was sad at that saying, and went away grieved: for he had great possessions.

Mark 10:17-22

You may have been taught in church or elsewhere that God wants you to be broke, to have nothing, to live in poverty. You may have been led to believe that in order to be a disciple of Christ you have to give away everything you own to the poor.

That is not what Jesus was saying to this rich young man. He told him to sell what he owned and give it away, and then to come and follow Him, only because He knew that this young man lacked something in his life. The thing he lacked was a sense of proper priorities.

This young man was rich because he had kept the commandments of the Lord all his life, and God had rewarded him handsomely. The problem was that he loved his money more than he did God. Jesus knew that unless he was willing to put God first, he would be of no use to the Kingdom.

The same is true of us. God wants us to have things — He is the One Who created them for us and Who gives them to us. But when we begin to put things ahead of God, when we begin to love the provisions more than the Provider, then we have a problem — just as this young man did.

It is not a matter of possessing, it is a matter of being possessed. It is not what we own that causes problems, it's what we love. Like this young man, unless we are willing to put God first, we can never be true disciples of the Lord Jesus Christ, no matter how much or how little we may possess.

Who Can Be Saved?

And Jesus looked round about, and saith unto his disciples, How hardly shall they that have riches enter into the kingdom of God!

And the disciples were astonished at his words. But Jesus answereth again, and saith unto them, Children, how hard is it for them that trust in riches to enter into the kingdom of God!

It is easier for a camel to go through the eye of a needle, than for a rich man to enter into the kingdom of God.

And they were astonished out of measure, saying among themselves, Who then can be saved?

And Jesus looking upon them saith, With men it is impossible, but not with God: for with God all things are possible.

Mark 10:23-27

The reason the disciples were so astonished at Jesus' words about how hard it is for a rich person to be saved is because they were prosperous men themselves. They knew that under the law, if a person was prosperous, it was a sign that He was faithful to God. What they were asking each other was, "If we can't be saved, then who can?"

Jesus' answer to their question was, "With men this is impossible, but not for God, because with God, nothing is impossible."

What He meant was, if a person allows his riches to come between him and the Lord, then it is impossible for him to enter the Kingdom of heaven.

Trust God, Not Riches

> **Charge them that are rich in this world, that they be not highminded, nor trust in uncertain riches, but in the living God, who giveth us richly all things to enjoy;**
>
> **That they do good, that they be rich in good works, ready to distribute, willing to communicate.**
>
> **1 Timothy 6:17,18**

The rich young man knew that he was blessed because he had been faithful to the Lord's commandments. Yet, he felt that he needed something else. What he needed was to learn to put God first, ahead of his possessions. That's why Jesus told him to get rid of them and follow Him. That way he would be totally dependent upon the Lord. If he had been willing to do that, he would have been blessed and prospered just as he was before, but this time he would have his priorities straight. He would put God first. His trust would be in the Lord rather than in his possessions, just as Paul instructed young Timothy to teach the people in his day.

Notice that Paul did not instruct Timothy to teach the rich that they should sell everything they own and give the proceeds to the poor. He just said to teach them that they should trust in God and not in their possessions, that they should be willing to share with others the good things that God had given to them.

That is what you and I are to do with the good things that God wants to pour out upon us as His beloved children. That is how we enter the realm of success — by trusting God and putting Him first in our lives.

9

Nine Steps to Success

Thus far we have been considering ways to get out of debt, to become debt free, to destroy the root of debt that is plaguing God's people and hampering the spread of His Kingdom throughout the earth.

In these last three chapters, we are going to discuss the nine steps to success. First, we will list these important steps, and then we will examine each of them in some detail.

The Nine Steps

1. *Have a vision.*
2. *Believe in your vision.*
3. *Conceive your vision in prayer.*
4. *Plan your vision.*
5. *Talk your vision.*
6. *Act upon the Word of God.*
7. *Pursue your vision with patience.*
8. *Take the limits off God.*
9. *Learn from the success of others.*

STEP 1: Have a vision.

> **Where there is no vision, the people perish: but he that keepeth the law, happy is he.**
>
> **Proverbs 29:18**

The first step in success is to have a vision, or to envision your future. If you want to achieve something in life, you must have a goal to accomplish, an objective to reach, an ideal to follow.

The poorest person in the world is not the one without a cent in his pocket. It is the one without a dream in his heart. The greatest tragedy is not that of having no money in your bank account. It is that of having no vision for your life.

If you have a vision, you will get the money it takes to fulfill it. When you are possessed of a dream, it will cause money and prosperity to come your way.

The Bible tells us that where there is no vision, the people perish. The word *perish* means to expire. If you have no vision, you will expire. But when you get a vision for your life, you will be inspired.

I am a man of vision, of inspiration. I am inspired every day to go up and not down. That should be your vision and inspiration.

Look to the Future in Confidence

I can do all things through Christ which strengtheneth me.

Philippians 4:13

Today is yesterday's future. What you did yesterday determines the quality of your today. And what you do today will determine the quality of your tomorrow. So if you want tomorrow to be better than today, you need to plan for it now. You need to have a dream, a vision of what you want your tomorrow to be like.

Today is the result of yesterday. If you didn't plan anything for today, there is a good chance that you don't have anything planned for tomorrow — or the day after tomorrow — or the day after that. Your days will go on, one after the other, each just like the one before it — until you decide to do something about your tomorrow by doing something about today.

Some people never plan anything. Some never plan to do anything, others never plan to *be* anything. They just live from one day to the next, just taking things as they come, just "going with the flow." No ship ever reached its destination by just drifting with the tide. If you want to get someplace, then you must have a definite goal and destination in mind. You must have a vision, and a plan to fulfill that vision.

I don't live by the philosophy that "whatever will be will be." I believe that whatever is planned will be. I don't just make the best of circumstances, I create my own circumstances. I don't just accept whatever happens, I cause things to happen. I confess every day with the Apostle Paul that I can do all things through Christ Who strengthens me.

I have a vision. I look to the future. I plan for that future.

So should you.

Have An Ideal

While we look not at the things which are seen, but at the things which are not seen: for the things which are seen are temporal; but the things which are not seen are eternal.

2 Corinthians 4:18

The success of your future lies in your ability to see beyond what is to what will be.

Robert Kennedy is often quoted as saying, "Some people look at things as they are and ask, why. I look at things as they could be and ask, why not?"

When I read about looking not at the things that are seen but at the things that are not seen, I think about Henry Ford, who worked in an automobile factory in a garage. Henry Ford came up with the idea of mass producing cars on an assembly line. In some twenty years, he went from a poverty-stricken laborer to one of the richest men in the world.

Henry Ford is an example of how one idea can change a person's whole life. One inspiration from God can cause you to go from rags to riches. One dream from the Lord can change you from a failure to a success.

I need an idea, a dream, an inspiration from God. I pray every day, "Oh, Lord, give me a vision, a plan. Change my life." I pray that because I know that prosperity does not come by chance, but by choice. I know that if I am going to be successful and prosperous tomorrow, then I must have a vision and a dream and a plan today.

Satan will not just let us walk into prosperity and success by chance, or just because we would like to. We have got to decide to be what we want to become, to have what we want to possess. We must make up our minds that we are going to succeed and that we will not let the enemy hinder us from achieving what the Lord has implanted in our hearts and minds.

Things don't just happen. They come about as a result of planning. But in order to plan, you must first know what you want to achieve. Before planning comes dreaming, envisioning, desiring.

I refuse to have anything in my life but prosperity and success. I refuse to be the tail. I refuse to be under. I refuse to be without, to have nothing, to be a nobody, because my God has made me to be somebody. I refuse even to associate with people who drag me down or belittle or discourage me. I refuse to stay around those who don't think much of me, because I know that as

I think, so am I. If I am to become on the outside what I think about on the inside, then I need to be around people and circumstances that raise my level of thought.

So do you.

Don't Look Back, Press Forward

> **Brethren, I count not myself to have apprehended: but this one thing I do, forgetting those things which are behind, and reaching forth unto those things which are before,**
>
> **I press toward the mark for the prize of the high calling of God in Christ Jesus.**
>
> **Philippians 3:13,14**

I refuse to look back. I refuse to review my past mistakes and failures. I refuse to talk negative — or to associate with others who talk negative, ignorant, or foolish. Even if it is a member of my own family who is doing so, I avoid that person, because I need a dream, a vision, an inspired ideal from God that will cause me to move ahead in life and fulfill the high calling that He has placed on my life.

The same is true of you. If you are ever to be a success, you need a vision — and a plan.

STEP 2: Believe in your vision.

> **...If thou canst believe, all things are possible to him that believeth.**
>
> **Mark 9:23**

If the dream or vision you have in your heart is believable, then it is achievable.

The Lord has assured us that whatever we can believe, we can achieve. If you have faith in the vision that God has given you, then with His help you will be able to fulfill it.

In my own case, I have the vision of reaching the entire state of Louisiana with the Gospel of Jesus Christ. I honestly believe that with the Lord's help, my people and I can do just that. I am fully persuaded and assured that my dream is possible.

Someone else may have it as his dream to own all the oil wells in the world. That is a dream or a vision, but it is not believable, especially when the person doesn't own even one well.

It is not enough to have a dream; that dream must be realizable.

Make sure that what you choose as a vision or goal is believable. The best way to do that is to go to the Lord and get the vision from Him. That way you can know that what you are dreaming can truly become reality.

Then once you have your God-given vision, have faith that the Lord will show you how to reach that inspired goal.

Have Faith in God

> **...Have faith in God.**
>
> **For verily I say unto you, That whosoever shall say unto this mountain, Be thou removed, and be thou cast into the sea; and shall not doubt in his heart, but shall believe that those things which he saith shall come to pass; he shall have whatsoever he saith.**
>
> **Therefore I say unto you, What things soever ye desire, when ye pray, believe that ye receive them, and ye shall have them.**
>
> **Mark 11:22-24**

Jesus taught us that if you and I would believe that those things that we say will come to pass, then we will have whatever we say.

The catch is that what we say must be believable. If something is believable, then when we pray and believe and speak, what we say will produce results.

That's what Paul meant when he said that he could do all things through Christ Who strengthened him. He did not mean that he could do just anything that came into his head. He meant that he could do whatever the Lord required of him. He meant that whatever the task, with the help of the Lord, he was equal to it.

The Living Bible version of Philippians 4:13 says:

> **...I can do everything God asks me to do with the help of Christ who gives me the strength and power.**

With the help of Christ Who strengthens and empowers you, you, too, can do everything that God asks you to do. You can accomplish your vision, fulfill your dream, achieve your goal — if that vision and dream and goal is one that was given to you by God. If it is, then it is something that you can truly believe in your heart.

The rule is: You can have whatever you say — if you can believe what you say. And in order to be able to believe what you say, what you say must be believable. And in order for it to be believable, it must come from God — not from your own imagination or fantasy or wishful thinking.

Get a vision that you can believe, and then believe in your vision.

STEP 3: Conceive your vision in prayer.

> **And this is the confidence that we have in him, that, if we ask any thing according to his will, he heareth us:**

> **And if we know that he hear us, whatsoever we ask, we know that we have the petitions that we desired of him.**
>
> **1 John 5:14,15**

Whatever the vision, it must be birthed in prayer.

When you have received a vision from the Lord, sometimes it may seem that it is never going to be fulfilled. It may seem that you will never see your desire come to pass. That is when you must hold fast to your faith, confident that the good work the Lord has begun in you, He will bring to completion. (Phil. 1:6.)

In order for Him to do that, however, you must do your part. And your part is to believe and conceive.

Believe and Conceive

Start seeing what you believe. Conceive it in your heart. Carry it through to fulfillment, just as an expectant mother carries her unborn child until the time for it to be born.

John tells us that if we know that God hears us when we pray, then we know that we will receive whatever we ask of Him. The problem is that many people don't know that God has heard them. The way to know is by praying in accordance with God's will. And the way to pray in accordance with God's will is to pray in accordance with His Word.

If we ask anything in accordance with God's will, His Word, He has promised to hear us and answer us. If you know that it is God's will for you to be healthy, based on His Word, then you can pray in confidence for divine health. The same is true for forgiveness, for salvation, or for prosperity and success.

When you pray, you don't need to wonder whether God hears you or not. You just need to find out what His will is for you and then pray for those things that you know He wants you to have.

And, as we have seen, God has made it abundantly clear that He wants all His children to prosper, and be healthy, even as our souls prosper. So your job is to pray God's will for you — which in this case is the fulfillment of the dream and vision that He Himself has placed in you. That is how you conceive and give birth to it.

Pray With All Kinds of Prayer

> **Praying always with all prayer and supplication in the Spirit, and watching thereunto with all perseverance. . . .**
>
> **Ephesians 6:18**

Paul tells us to pray always, and with all kinds of prayer.

There are several types of prayer that will help you to believe, conceive and bring forth your vision:

*Prayer of Faith — The prayer of petition, the prayer to change things (Matthew 21:22; Mark 11:24). This prayer is always to be based on God's revealed will in His Word.

*Prayer of Thanksgiving and Praise — (Acts 13:2; Acts 16:25,26; Luke 24:52,53). Praise and thank God every day for answered prayer. The book of Psalms is filled with praise and thanksgiving to God for His blessings and goodness. Start thanking God for debt cancellation.

*Prayer in the Spirit — (1 Corinthians 14:14,15; Jude 20). Praying in tongues.

*Prayer of Binding and Loosing — Bind the spirit of debt, and loose the spirit of prosperity. **'I tell you**

the truth, whatever you bind on earth will be bound in heaven, and whatever you loose on earth will be loosed in heaven' (Matthew 18:18, NIV).

Fight the Good Fight of Faith

> **For we wrestle not against flesh and blood, but against principalities, against powers, against the rulers of the darkness of this world, against spiritual wickedness in high places.**
>
> **Ephesians 6:12**

As you hold fast to the vision that God has given you, remember that you are engaged in spiritual warfare. You must fight the good fight of faith until you see the manifestation of what you are believing, what you have conceived in your heart.

The enemy of your soul will try to keep you from fulfilling your divine call and mission. That's why you must be firm in your commitment.

The Lord has said that *the wealth of the sinner is laid up for the just.* (Prov. 13:22.) We are coming into that inheritance in these last days. That's why Satan and his demons are attacking us constantly, to keep us from receiving all that God wants to place in our hands in order to establish His covenant in the earth and to spread His Kingdom around the world.

Pray Without Ceasing

> **Pray without ceasing.**
>
> **1 Thessalonians 5:17**

Just remain constant. Pray without ceasing, **be instant in season** [and]**, out of season.** (2 Tim. 4:2.)

Don't be moved by what you see. Don't be concerned with what others around you are saying or doing. Don't be bothered by the fact that you seem to be dependent upon other people for your welfare.

Man may determine your salary, but God determines your income.

It is God Who determines what comes into your life — not man. He decides the amount of your increase. Man may try to set limits on you, but it is God Who gives you the power and the ability to get wealth, just as it is God Who gives you ideas, and dreams, and visions.

In Joel 2:28, we read that in the last days old men shall dream dreams and young men shall see visions. I am just at the right age to see a lot of visions. You may be at the age where you are beginning to dream dreams. Once you have received a dream or a vision from the Lord, hang on to it with all your might.

Stand on the Word of God. Pray the prayer of binding and loosing. Pray the prayer of petition. Pray the prayer of thanksgiving and praise. Hold fast in prayer until you see the final fulfillment of your God-given dream or vision.

Whatever God has called you to do, whatever your dream or vision, conceive and give birth to it in prayer.

10
The Four Ds of Success

We have been examining the nine steps to success, which is guaranteed by the Lord to those who are willing and obedient to follow His plan and keep His command. All of these steps can be summarized into four attributes, which I call the Four Ds of Success:

1. *Determination.*

If you want to be successful, then you must be determined to be successful. It is not enough simply to wish and want. You must set your mind to accomplish your desires by determined effort.

2. *Decision.*

Success requires decisiveness. No one ever became a success by chance. If you want to succeed in life, then you must learn to make decisions and then see those decisions through to fulfillment.

3. *Diligence.*

Only those who are committed enough to stick to their plan will ever achieve anything of lasting value in this life. Nothing is more important for success than the ability to apply oneself to a task until it is completed.

4. *Discipline.*

Another word for *discipline* is self-control. If you want to achieve your goals in life, then you must be willing to make sacrifices, personal sacrifices. You must be willing to give up the good in order to have the best. God's blessings are for the dedicated, the committed, those who are willing to forego present gratification for future satisfaction.

Make a decision, be determined to back that decision, be diligent to stick to your decision, and then be disciplined to apply yourself daily to the task that decision demands. If you will do these things — be decisive, determined, diligent and disciplined — then with the help of God, sooner or later you *will* succeed.

Go for it!

STEP 4: Plan your vision.

> **Any enterprise is built by wise planning, becomes strong through common sense, and profits wonderfully by keeping abreast of the facts.**
>
> **Proverbs 24:3,4, TLB**

If you are to succeed in fulfilling your vision, in carrying out your plan, then you need to get organized. Any man or woman who will not plan and organize is destined for failure. Whatever you undertake to do in life will require wise planning, common sense and keeping abreast of the facts.

I have seen people in business who are terrible managers. They have no plan for their business, no organization for their activities. They have no records of the past, no accounts for the present, and no budget for the future. They just operate as they live — off the top of their heads or by the seat of their britches. That is not wise stewardship of God's investment.

If you have a small personal business, for example, then you should keep a reliable accounting of your income, expenses, taxes, employee wage payments and other financial matters. You should have some established procedure for keeping up with and taking care of tools and equipment, inventories and supplies. You should have a detailed operating budget for the year and an estimated growth plan for the years to come. You should know where you are going and how you are going to get there, step by step.

That is the way to prosper, by taking things one step at a time. You must realize and accept that God is not going to make you a multi-millionaire tomorrow. You didn't get into your current financial mess overnight, and you won't get out of it overnight.

You can get debt free, but it will probably take some time — perhaps months or even years, as in my own case. God did not miraculously cancel my debt. He can do that, and sometimes He may choose to do so, but that is not the norm.

Write the Vision

> **...Write the vision, and make it plain upon tables, that he may run that readeth it.**
>
> **Habakkuk 2:2**

The Lord told the Prophet Habakkuk to write the vision He was giving him, to make it plain upon tablets so that whoever read it could carry it out. That is good advice for us today.

If you have received a vision from the Lord, write it down. Organize it into believable, achievable steps. Be realistic in your planning. If you are beginning an automobile body shop, don't make it your goal to bring in a million dollars the first year of operation — especially if there are just you and your brother with two hammers and two cans of paint!

Such a goal is not believable even to you. Start out with a realistic goal of clearing five or ten thousand dollars after expenses. Start with a goal you can reach.

After you have attained that objective, then stretch a bit more. Plan a little higher. Make a little greater effort, a little larger investment.

But you must also be aware that as soon as you start to make progress toward your goals, the devil will come at you to try to make you fail. That's why you must write down your vision so you can keep it in front of your eyes and in your heart. Read it over and over, every day, reminding yourself that it was given to you by God. Because even with the help and encouragement of the Lord, there will come times when you will be tempted to give up. That's when you must remember that **we walk by faith, not by sight.** (2 Cor. 5:7.)

If we walked by sight and not by faith, I would have given up long ago. So would you. But just as we look to the written Word of the Lord to renew our minds and to keep our spirits revived, so we need to be able to look at our own personal goals and visions to keep from faltering and failing.

The Vision Will Speak

> **For the vision is yet for an appointed time, but at the end it shall speak, and not lie: though it tarry, wait for it; because it will surely come, it will not tarry.**
>
> **Habakkuk 2:3**

Write down not only the vision or goal or objective, also write down the steps that you are going to take to reach it.

In this verse, the Lord is telling us that we must be patient if we are to see our vision fulfilled. We must continue to follow our plan, day after day, month after month, year after year, if need be, until we see it come to pass — even though it may seem that day will never come.

In Galatians 6:9, the Apostle Paul exhorts us not to become weary in well-doing, assuring us that we will reap if we faint not. In Luke 18:1, we read that Jesus **...spake a parable unto them to this end, that men ought always to pray, and not to faint.**

Don't faint. Don't quit. If God has given you a vision, take that vision and draw up a plan to fulfill it. Then stay with that plan. Follow through with it. Organize your activities so that step by step, day by day, you are making progress toward your goal. Always know where you are, where you came from, and where you're going.

If you are in business, keep up with how much you are spending, how much you are making, and how much you need to invest to reach each succeeding goal. Use wisdom and, especially, common sense. It may be rough, but in the end, you will succeed.

One translation of Habakkuk 2:3 says that the vision will speak for itself. If you are decisive, determined, diligent and disciplined, one day you will see your vision become reality. Then it will speak for itself. In the meantime, you must speak for it.

STEP 5: Talk your vision.

> **Death and life are in the power of the tongue: and they that love it shall eat the fruit thereof.**
>
> **Proverbs 18:21**

Talk your vision. Confess it. By speaking the Word of God, you release the ability of the Lord to work for you.

To *confess* means to speak or declare what is believed. Speak what you believe. Your words release what is in your spirit. Start talking your vision. Don't associate with people who don't believe in you or your God-given vision.

Confession brings faith. It causes your faith to become stronger. When you speak your vision out of your mouth, it creates that for which you are believing God.

The writer of Proverbs tells us that death and life are in the power of the tongue, and that those who love it will eat the fruit of it. That means whatever we say is what we will have. That's why it is important to talk our desires and not our fears, to discuss our goals and objectives and not our failures and errors.

Don't dwell on the negative. Be positive. Don't talk about things you don't want to happen. Use your confession to change things that are not to things that are, to alter situations from bad to good, to transform negatives into positives, to turn adversity into prosperity, to create physical reality out of spiritual inspiration.

The Word Is Nigh Thee

> **But what saith it? The word is nigh thee, even in thy mouth, and in thy heart: that is, the word of faith, which we preach.**
>
> **Romans 10:8**

The mouth and the heart must go together. If you are not fulfilling your vision, it may be because you are saying things with your mouth that you do not really believe in your heart.

The Bible teaches, **. . . let the weak say, I am strong** (Joel 3:10). Instead of crying and feeling weak, you must begin to believe and confess that you are strong. If you truly believe in your heart what you say with your mouth, one day it will come true. You will be strong, just as you have believed and confessed.

That's why you should believe and confess that you can do all things through Christ Who strengthens you (Phil. 4:13), that you are more than a conqueror in Him (Rom. 8:37), that you are blessed of the Lord, the head and not the tail, above and not beneath, that God prospers everything you put your hand to (Deut. 28:1-13), that your every need is supplied by Him through the riches of Christ Jesus (Phil. 4:19).

Anyone can praise God in the good times. It is only when things are going bad that you have to stand against weakness and fear and temptation. That's the time that you need to be able to look at your vision and to hold fast to it because you know that God is faithful to what He has promised. (Heb. 10:23.)

Like Abraham, you must learn to hope against hope, to be obedient in spite of the way things look, to walk by faith and not by sight, to speak the Word with your mouth and believe it in your heart.

The Power of God

> **For I am not ashamed of the gospel of Christ: for it is the power of God...to every one that believeth....**
>
> **Romans 1:16**

You must not be ashamed of the Word of God. You must be as quick to speak it out of your mouth as you are to believe it in your heart. You must confess the Word of the Lord before men just as you confess the Lord Himself before men. (Mark 8:38.)

Speak the Word. Talk the Word. Do it on a daily basis. The Word of God is power. It has the ability to produce exactly what it says — when you speak it.

Speak your vision, and watch it come to pass in your life.

STEP 6: Act upon the Word of God.

But be ye doers of the word, and not hearers only, deceiving your own selves.

James 1:22

Act on the Word. You can never expect the Word of God to produce what you desire unless you are willing to put it into action in your daily life.

The Word of the Lord is not a magic formula that makes everything happen just as we want it to. God has told us what He desires and plans for us, and what we are to do to help bring it to pass. Our job and responsibility is to take the Word, that message from the Lord, and put it into daily practice so that together with Him we can bring about what He wills in every situation of life.

We must complete every step and in the order prescribed. If we try to jump directly from having a vision to acting on God's Word, without going through the entire process, we will fail. By the same token, if we try to jump directly from believing that our vision is possible to planning it, without following through on the speaking and acting, then we will be disappointed in the results.

You may have had a vision at one time. But Satan came and stole it away from you — maybe before you even knew it was there. The Bible says that when a person receives the Word, immediately the enemy comes to steal from him what he has received. (Mark 4:15.) That's why once you have received the Word, the vision, you must hold it in your mind and heart, speaking it from your mouth, and acting on it — so that you will not lose it.

Step Out in Faith

And in the fourth watch of the night Jesus went unto them, walking on the sea.

And when the disciples saw him walking on the sea, they were troubled, saying, It is a spirit; and they cried out for fear.

But straightway Jesus spake unto them, saying, Be of good cheer; it is I; be not afraid.

And Peter answered him and said, Lord, if it be thou, bid me come unto thee on the water.

And he said, Come. And when Peter was come down out of the ship, he walked on the water, to go to Jesus.

But when he saw the wind boisterous, he was afraid; and beginning to sink, he cried, saying, Lord, save me.

And immediately Jesus stretched forth his hand, and caught him, and said unto him, O thou of little faith, wherefore didst thou doubt?

Matthew 14:25-31

I have a vision. I see myself on radio and television stations all over this nation and around the world. I picture myself ministering for the Lord and blessing many people. I have received that vision. I have given it birth in my spirit. I have planned it and confessed it. Now it is time to act on it. Now I must take some positive steps to implement that vision, to see it actually become reality.

When the time comes to buy broadcast time, I can't do as Peter did in this story. I can't look around and get frightened. I can't suddenly back out, saying, "Lord, I'm scared. I know You have given me this vision, that You have called me to fulfill this call and reach these people for You, but I just can't do it. I'm afraid I'll fail."

Now is not the time to doubt and fear. If we do, we will sink. Now is the time to act on the Word of the Lord. If we do, we will be successful.

Act on the Word of the Lord. If you say that you see your family successful, your marriage successful, your business successful, then you ought to start acting like a successful parent, a successful spouse, a successful business person. If you say you see yourself sweet and kind and loving, then you need to begin to act that way. If you say you see yourself debt free, then you should start paying off what you owe. Quit charging things. Quit running up bills at the store or on your credit card. Start saying no to your impulse to buy, buy, buy. Don't even go to those places where you know you will be tempted to purchase on credit things you know you don't need and can't afford.

Set your goals high, and then begin to act on the vision that you have established in your heart. The Lord will help you as you apply the Four D's of Success: determination, decision, diligence and discipline.

11
The Final Word

After you have got your vision in your spirit, you believe it in your heart, conceive it in your prayers, talk it with your mouth and act upon it in faith, then it is time to take the final three steps to ultimate success.

STEP 7: Pursue your vision with patience.

> **Cast not away therefore your confidence, which hath great recompence of reward.**
>
> **For ye have need of patience, that, after ye have done the will of God, ye might receive the promise.**
>
> **Hebrews 10:35,36**

After you have acted on the Word of God, you need patience to see it come to pass.

Don't throw away your confidence. Hold on to it. If you are believing God to become debt free, then give Him the time He needs to bring that to pass. Do your part by making every effort to start paying off what you owe yourself. Take those bills one at a time and start reducing them down. It took my wife and me ten years to get out of our debt, so it may take a while for you.

Isaiah says of the Lord: **Thou will keep him in perfect peace, whose mind is stayed on thee: because he trusteth in thee** (Is. 26:3). In Acts 20:24, Paul wrote that he was faced with hardship and difficulty on every side, but that none of those things moved him.

That is the way you must be in your situation. Whatever your vision, put your trust in the Lord so that He may keep you in His perfect peace. Don't allow yourself to be moved by the way things look or by the amount of time it may take to set them straight. Be patient to work at it. Your dream will come to pass, but it cannot be rushed. Whatever happens, you must be steadfast, immovable, not becoming weary in well-doing, knowing that you will reap if you faint not. (Gal. 6:9.)

Be Ye Stedfast, Unmoveable

> **Therefore, my beloved brethren, be ye stedfast, unmoveable, always abounding in the work of the Lord, forasmuch as ye know that your labour is not in vain in the Lord.**
>
> **1 Corinthians 15:58**

This verse has a double message. First, we are to be steadfast and immovable.

The word *steadfast* means to be constantly or continually the same, having self-control. When you have a dream, you don't need to be wild and uncontrolled. A person who cannot or will not control himself will ultimately and inevitably fail.

The word *immovable* means incapable of being moved. But we see that though we cannot be moved by outside forces, that does not mean that we are not to move ourselves. While we are to be steady, we are not to be idle. We are to be abounding in the work of the Lord.

Some sports figure has said that all good things come to those who wait — provided they hustle while they wait. That is the message of this verse.

We are not just to sit and do nothing as we wait for the blessing of the Lord to fall upon us out of heaven. If we want to receive, we must do more than just believe, or just keep repeating that we believe. We must *do* something to translate our belief into reality.

Notice that while we are being steadfast and immovable, we are to be abounding in the work of the Lord, we are to be laboring. If we are to be blessed, then we must *work.*

We can't just hear a message and then expect it to come to pass in our lives without any effort on our part. We must act upon the Word we receive. We must be doers of the Word, and not just hearers. We must apply ourselves to *do* the work of the Lord, allowing patience to have her perfect work in us.

Be Patient and Persevere

> **But let patience have her perfect work, that ye may be perfect and entire, wanting nothing.**
>
> **James 1:4**

One of the characteristics of patience is emotional control. When you have a dream, you must learn to keep your emotions in check. Don't be so quick to take offense or to be moved by outside events or other people. The devil will take advantage of anyone who does not control his inward emotions and outward reactions.

The *New International Bible* version of this verse says: **Perseverance must finish its work so that you may be mature and complete, not lacking anything.**

When you have a vision, you must wait upon that vision, but you must do more than just wait. To patience must be added perseverance. You must not only give the Lord time to work, you must work yourself. That may mean getting a job, or a better job, or even taking on an extra job. It may mean working longer hours or spending less time on personal pleasures and unproductive pastimes. Whatever the Lord reveals for you to do to bring your vision to pass, apply yourself to that task with all your heart. Abound in the work of the Lord, in His labor, allowing patience and perseverance to have their perfect work in you, so that you may become mature and complete, lacking nothing.

Don't look to a minister or church to lay hands on you and miraculously cancel your debts. It doesn't work that way. It takes time and effort to get out of debt. You and your spouse must sit down and make a realistic plan for controlling your spending and paying off those you owe. You are going to have to be willing to say no to some things you would like to have but can't afford. You are going to have to start tithing and giving offerings to the Lord, even if that means reducing the amount you spend on yourself and your own desires. You are going to have to exercise diligence and patience and perseverance. But in the end, it will be rewarded. God has said so.

STEP 8: Take the limits off God.

> **Is any thing too hard for the Lord?**
>
> **Genesis 18:14**

You and I serve a big God, One Who is able to perform what He has promised. (Rom. 4:21.)

When you get your vision, take the limits off God. You can go as high as you believe you can go. You can do everything He asks you to do with the help of Jesus Christ Who gives you the strength and power. (Phil. 4:13, TLB.)

Because God has no limits, you have no limits — if you love God and are fitting in with His plans. (Rom. 8:28, TLB.)

At the Appointed Time

...At the time appointed I will return unto thee, according to the time of life, and Sarah shall have a son.

Genesis 18:14

Does that phrase, "at the time appointed" sound familiar? Remember what the Lord told the prophet in Habakkuk 2:2,3:

...Write the vision, and make it plain upon tables, that he may run that readeth it. For the vision is yet for an appointed time....

That is God's Word to you as much as it was to Habakkuk. You have a time and a season.

That's why it is so important that you not be concerned about what others may think or say or do. If you will do right, if you will keep your heart right before the Lord, if you will take God at His Word, if you will take the limits off the Lord, your vision will be fulfilled — at the appointed time.

STEP 9: Learn from the success of others.

And what shall I more say? for the time would fail me to tell of Gedeon, and of Barak, and of Samson, and of Jephthae; of David also, and Samuel, and of the prophets:

Who through faith subdued kingdoms, wrought righteousness, obtained promises, stopped the mouths of lions,

Quenched the violence of fire, escaped the edge of the sword, out of weakness were made strong, waxed valiant in fight, turned to flight the armies of the aliens.

> **Women received their dead raised to life again. . . .**
>
> **Hebrews 11:32-35**

Learn from the success of others. Associate with people who have been successful, people who think and talk and act positive, people who are living the way you want to live.

If you want to be debt free, then associate with those who owe no one anything except the debt of love. (Rom. 13:8.) Get around people who have a vision and who are seeing their vision become reality. That way you will begin to think and talk and act success.

If your vision is to have a happy marriage and family and home, don't spend time with those who are always complaining about their spouse or their children or their relatives.

If your vision is to be a success in business, don't hang around with losers. Spend time with those people whose lives are a testimony to the grace and love and abundance of God.

When I travel, I visit successful churches and ministries. I go to observe, to learn, to be inspired, to catch a glimpse of what I want to be and to do and to have.

Imitate Those Who Imitate Christ

> **Join with others in following my example, brothers, and take note of those who live according to the pattern we gave you.**
>
> **Philippians 3:17, NIV**

Begin to act like those you admire and respect. I tell my people, "Fake it until you make it." I don't mean by that that they should be hypocrites. I mean that they should find good role models to emulate and imitate, that they should begin to live up to the standards that they have set for themselves. I mean that, like faithful Abraham, in the face of difficulty and doubt and adversity, they should hope against hope. That no matter what comes, they should live as if what they are believing were factual reality. That they should see themselves as winners and not as losers.

If you want to see your vision fulfilled, then begin to act as if it were already true in your life.

Wherever you may be at the moment, maybe God has placed you there for a purpose. God needs you on that job. Be submissive to His leading and obedient to His will, and "at the appointed time" He will guide you into the place of honor and influence that you should occupy, just as He did with Joseph.

In the meantime, think and talk and look and act like the person you want to become — and one day you will discover that you have become that person!

Be Not Idle, But Work

> **For you yourselves know how you ought to follow our example. We were not idle when we were with you, nor did we eat anyone's food without paying for it. On the contrary, we worked night and day, laboring and toiling so that we would not be a burden to any of you. We did this, not because we do not have the right to such help, but in order to make ourselves a model for you to follow.**
>
> **2 Thessalonians 3:7-9, NIV**

We serve a successful God, a big God, a God Who can meet all of our needs. Learn to follow the example of those who live by His standards; those who work hard; those who labor and toil so they will not be a burden on society, their family, their church, or their government; those who want to be models for others to follow; those who are a success and not a failure; those who are part of the solution and not the problem.

Learn From Your Own Successes

And David said to Saul, Let no man's heart fail because of him; thy servant will go and fight with this Philistine.

And Saul said to David, Thou art not able to go against this Philistine to fight with him: for thou art but a youth, and he a man of war from his youth.

And David said unto Saul, Thy servant kept his father's sheep, and there came a lion, and a bear, and took a lamb out of the flock:

And I went out after him, and smote him, and delivered it out of his mouth: and when he arose against me, I caught him by his beard, and smote him, and slew him.

Thy servant slew both the lion and the bear: and this uncircumcised Philistine shall be as one of them, seeing he hath defied the armies of the living God.

David said moreover, The Lord that delivered me out of the paw of the lion, and out of the paw of the bear, he will deliver me out of the hand of this Philistine. And Saul said unto David, Go, and the Lord be with thee.

1 Samuel 17:32-37

Learn from the success of others, and learn from your own successes.

Do as David did and review your past. Look back and remember the times that God brought you through difficulty and hardship. Recall how He saved you and healed you and provided for you time after time. Rehearse how He forgave and restored you when you had fallen, how He gave you a new and better job when you had been laid off, how He lifted you up from the miry clay, set your feet on a rock, established your going and put a new song of praise and thanksgiving in your mouth.

God has not changed. He is **the same yesterday, and today, and for ever** (Heb. 13:8). With His help and guidance and provision, you will be delivered out of the hand of the enemy, you will overcome your Goliath — whatever that may be.

With God on your side, you will not fail. You will prosper. You will succeed.

Go, and the Lord be with you.